# *DeMar DeRozan: The Inspiring Story of One of Basketball's Star Shooting Guards*

An Unauthorized Biography

By: Clayton Geoffreys

Copyright © 2018 by Calvintir Books, LLC

All rights reserved. Neither this book nor any portion thereof may be reproduced or used in any manner whatsoever without the express written permission. Published in the United States of America.

**Disclaimer**: The following book is for entertainment and informational purposes only. The information presented is without contract or any type of guarantee assurance. While every caution has been taken to provide accurate and current information, it is solely the reader's responsibility to check all information contained in this article before relying upon it. Neither the author nor publisher can be held accountable for any errors or omissions.

Under no circumstances will any legal responsibility or blame be held against the author or publisher for any reparation, damages, or monetary loss due to the information presented, either directly or indirectly. This book is not intended as legal or medical advice. If any such specialized advice is needed, seek a qualified individual for help.

Trademarks are used without permission. Use of the trademark is not authorized by, associated with, or sponsored by the trademark owners. All trademarks and brands used within this book are used with no intent to infringe on the trademark owners and only used for clarifying purposes.

This book is not sponsored by or affiliated with the National Basketball Association, its teams, the players, or anyone involved with them.

Visit my website at www.claytongeoffreys.com
Cover photo by Keith Allison is licensed under CC BY 2.0 / modified from original

# Table of Contents

Foreword ............................................................................... 1

Introduction .......................................................................... 3

Chapter 1: Childhood and Early Life ................................... 8

Chapter 2: High School Career ........................................... 11

Chapter 3: College Career ................................................... 14

Chapter 4: NBA Career ....................................................... 18

    Getting Drafted ............................................................... 18

    The Rookie Campaign .................................................... 24

    The Development Years ................................................. 29

    Teaming Up with Kyle Lowry, the Rudy Gay Experiment ...................................................................... 36

    First All-Star Season, Playoff Debut ............................. 40

    Injury Struggles, Lowry's Evolution into an All-Star .... 50

    Breaking Through to the Conference Finals ................. 57

    The Road to Becoming Elite .......................................... 73

The Final Year in Toronto ................................................. 85

The Trade to San Antonio ................................................ 96

Chapter 5: International Career ......................................... 101

Chapter 6: Personal Life .................................................... 103

Chapter 7: Impact on Basketball ....................................... 105

Chapter 8: Legacy and Future ........................................... 107

Final Word/About the Author ........................................... 113

References .......................................................................... 116

# Foreword

Drafted ninth overall by the Toronto Raptors in the 2009 NBA draft, DeMar DeRozan has quickly emerged as a premier shooting guard in the NBA. While still in the prime of his career, DeRozan has already accomplished much to be proud of, including participating as a member of both the 2014 World Cup and 2016 Summer Olympics. DeRozan has been a highly-touted shooting guard since high school, as he was one of the top three recruits in his graduating class. After one year at the University of Southern California, DeMar declared for the NBA draft and began his professional career. He has played a pivotal role in the emergence of the Toronto Raptors as a force in the Eastern Conference. In the summer of 2018, the Raptors decided to shake things up by trading DeMar for Kawhi Leonard. Now, DeMar has a new opportunity to start a new chapter with the legendary Spurs franchise. Thank you for purchasing *DeMar DeRozan: The Inspiring Story of One of Basketball's Star Shooting Guards*. In this unauthorized biography, we will learn DeMar DeRozan's incredible life story and impact on the game of basketball. Hope you enjoy and if you do, please do not forget to leave a review!

Also, check out my website at claytongeoffreys.com to join my exclusive list where I let you know about my latest books. To thank you for your purchase, you can go to my site to download a free copy of *33 Life Lessons: Success Principles, Career Advice & Habits of Successful People*. In the book, you'll learn from some of the greatest thought leaders of different industries on what it takes to become successful and how to live a great life.

Cheers,

*Clayton Geoffreys*

*Visit me at www.claytongeoffreys.com*

# Introduction

The shooting guard position has always been one of the more difficult spots to play in the NBA. Shooting guards are required to be among the best scorers on their team since their primary role of the team is to, of course, shoot and make their shots. While scoring the ball may not sound like the most difficult task, what makes the shooting guard a difficult position in the NBA is the level of skill required to be elite.

As far as the history of the league is concerned, there have not been as many great shooting guards as centers, point guards, and forwards due to the relative difficulty the position requires for the player to be elite. But even though there have not been many great shooting guards in the NBA's history, the best of the best happen to be those that play that position.

Since the dawn of the league, the first great shooting guard was the NBA logo himself, Jerry West. Then there came guys like George Gervin and Pete Maravich during the dark 70's era of the league. During the 80's and 90's, Reggie Miller and Clyde Drexler dominated the position. Those that came after them were Kobe Bryant, Ray Allen, Vince Carter, and Dwyane Wade. Michael Jordan, the greatest player to have ever played the game, is known as a shooting guard. There have not been a lot of great shooting guards, but they were always the best of their respective eras.

What made those great shooting guards truly elite were combinations of factors that not a lot of players are gifted with. The best shooting guards always had size. Gervin, MJ, Drexler, Carter, and Kobe were all listed as at least 6'6". Size was always a factor when it came to becoming an elite shooting guard. Then there is also athleticism. The great shooting guards were always among the most athletic players in the league. Those that have dominated the position could glide in the air, hang near the rim, and dunk over bigger defenders.

And while any shooting guard can be distinguished and athletic, what truly makes one great is the level of skill required at that position. The best shooting guards are not only required to handle the ball like a point guard but are also supposed to have an arsenal of scoring moves from all spots on the floor whether it was beyond the three-point arc, within the perimeter, or near the basket. Elite shooting guards are considered complete scorers as far as physical attributes and skills are concerned.

Since the shooting guard may be the most difficult position to play in the NBA, there are not a lot of great ones in today's league. But there is a certain player that has all the makings of a truly elite shooting guard. At 6'7", he has the size to score and bully smaller defenders. With a vertical leap of nearly 40 inches, he is among the most athletic players at his position. And with an array of slashing and finishing moves and perimeter skills, he has all the tools to put points up on the board in a hurry. That player DeMar DeRozan.

Like most shooting guards before him, it took DeMar DeRozan some time before he fully transformed into an elite player in the NBA. He came into the league with all the athleticism in his 6'7" frame. He was a raw athlete, though he had a lot of potential to be a star. A rebuilding Toronto Raptors team was patient with DeRozan as the young guard took his time to fully transform into a star that had a complete array of scoring skills.

Once DeMar DeRozan learned to harness his athleticism and developed all-around scoring skills, he became an unstoppable perimeter and slashing threat for a Toronto Raptors team that had become reliant on the wingman for offense and leadership. Along with Kyle Lowry, DeRozan gave the Toronto Raptors one of the best backcourts in the league as far as scoring is concerned.

As DeRozan improved year by year, the Toronto Raptors also grew as a franchise. Despite having all-time great players such as Vince Carter and Chris Bosh, the Raptors never got far into the playoffs until DeMar DeRozan took them to the Eastern Conference Finals in 2016 for the first time in history. Though he had a lot of flair in his game, especially when it came to slashing and finishing at the basket, DeRozan has always been a quiet and humble operator that proved to be one of the better players in Raptors history. He silently led the way for his team to reach the franchise's deepest playoff run while also racking up enough points to become the Raptors' all-time leading scorer.

Then, in 2018, he would lead the Toronto Raptors to the best record in the East and to a franchise record of 59 wins in a single season. No Raptors great, not even Vince Carter or Chris Bosh, has ever done that in the past. Nevertheless, DeMar DeRozan would find himself losing once again to LeBron James and the Cleveland Cavaliers in the playoffs as the Raptors' efforts to get the top seed had gone to smoke.

If there ever was a knock to DeMar DeRozan's stint in Toronto, it was that he was always unable to defeat LeBron James in the playoffs. As good as he is as a player and as great as he has been for the Raptors, he has never led his team past King James. This, among other things, was one of the reasons why the Toronto Raptors realized they needed to move forward by trading away DeMar DeRozan to the San Antonio Spurs in exchange for Kawhi Leonard. But getting traded for another star does not diminish DeRozan's status as one of the best wingmen in the league.

Because DeMar DeRozan is still in the prime of his physical and athletic capabilities, he is still expected to improve more as a player and leader. He has all the makings and tools to become an all-time great at the shooting guard position. When gliding in the air, he looks like Drexler. When finishing at the basket, he is Jordan-esque. And when it came down to hitting midrange turnaround jumpers, it seems as though he yells "Kobe" when the shots hit the bottom of the rim. As he continues to rise through the ranks of the great shooting guards in league history, DeMar DeRozan is also expected to grow even more under Gregg Popovich's tutelage in San Antonio. And if the stars align, the Spurs might have their new franchise star in DeRozan.

# Chapter 1: Childhood and Early Life

DeMar DeRozan was born on August 7, 1989, in Compton, California to parents Frank and Diane DeRozan. DeMar was a lucky baby in a marriage that grew for five years before he was born. Nobody thought that the union between Frank and Diane would ever bear a child. Fibroids, which are abnormal growths, were found in Diane's uterus. It was almost impossible for her to carry a child for her husband, but she did. Out came DeMar, a nine-pound baby nicknamed the "Blessed One" by his grandmother because he was born under impossible circumstances.[i] His birth was not the only blessing he and his family would receive in their respective lives.

DeMar DeRozan would be raised in Compton under watchful eyes in a tough neighborhood. After all, his late uncle Lemar, who he was named after, was killed at the early age of 20 in the middle of a successful college football career. Another uncle, Kevin, was also gunned down in the same neighborhood. This was the reason why his family kept a constant watch over him.

DeMar's father Frank, who would work as a videographer during his son's formative years, used to be a football star himself, having played for the San Diego Chargers for a short while. With football backgrounds in both his parents' sides of the family, DeMar DeRozan obviously had the makings of a future athletic freak. His NBA career would be a testament to those athletic roots. But even with his athletic genes, DeRozan would always stand by the words of his parents. His mother and father worked hard to get to where they were. The lesson he got from his folks was that he had to work for everything he wanted to achieve since it would never be handed to you if you did not strived hard for it in the first place.[ii]

Growing up in California during the late 90's and the early 2000's, nobody would ever wonder why DeMar DeRozan's favorite basketball icon was Kobe Bryant of the Los Angeles Lakers. He was merely 15 miles away from the Staples Center where the Lakers played their home games. He was seven years old when he saw Kobe Bryant, a rookie back then, airball crucial baskets in Game 5 of the Lakers' first-round loss to the Utah Jazz in the 1997 NBA playoffs.[iii] Even at that young age and Kobe's relative youth and inexperience in the NBA, DeMar DeRozan had already come to admire the future Hall of Famer. After that, he learned Bryant's moves and emulated his skills. DeRozan would try to copy Kobe Bryant's offensive arsenal.

But DeMar was obviously a better athlete than Kobe ever was at a young age. At 12 years old, he had already made his first dunk. But it was not a simple dunk. He was dunking over his father, a huge 6'4" man who played linebacker back in his football days. News quickly spread about DeRozan's early athletic pedigree. He was already getting the attention of several high school programs in Compton.

# Chapter 2: High School Career

DeMar DeRozan was originally supposed to attend Dominguez High School in Compton because of the national championship background surrounding it. The school was also able to produce NBA players such as Tayshaun Prince and Brandon Jennings, who would both have respectable careers in the professional league. Even Frank DeRozan wanted his son to attend Dominguez. But instead, DeMar would go to Compton High School, which was right across from the DeRozan residence. His mission was to make Compton High School relevant.

Back then, two schools dominated the Compton landscape of prep basketball. The first was Dominguez, which had produced several NBA players on their way to championships. The second was Centennial High School, where another future NBA player, Aaron Afflalo, once dominated. DeMar DeRozan was determined to lead his school to greatness, averaging 26 points as a freshman. He would lead Compton High School to a playoff appearance after years of not getting that far.

At the tender age of 14, DeMar DeRozan honed his skills by playing in the Drew League. Back then, older future NBA players such as Baron Davis and Dorell Wright were dominating the Drew League. But it did not hinder the 14-year-old from trying to become a better player against bigger, older, and more experienced competition. He liked the competition in the Drew League since grown men did not care whether they were playing against a teenager such as him.[iv]

As his high school years went by, there were many moments when DeMar DeRozan was courted by the rival high school teams to transfer to their program. After all, Compton High School was not as decorated as Dominguez and Crossroads. Even the teachers, parents, and coaches back at Compton High expressed their concerns about the possibility of DeRozan leaving for greener pastures.

Instead, DeMar DeRozan stayed loyal. He was true to his word when he said that he wanted Compton to be a local powerhouse. He wanted his school to become relevant. Instead of joining programs that had better players and coaches, he relished the competition of playing against the local rivals. DeRozan, like his idol Kobe Bryant, was fuelled by the passion of going up against better opponents. He would make both Dominguez and Crossroads stepping stones in winning the Huntington Beach Ocean View Championship in his junior year where he averaged 22.3 points and 7.8 rebounds throughout the year. He would also lead his team to a Moore League title that season.

It was also around that age in his high school career when DeMar DeRozan first formed a bond with Kobe Bryant. DeMar was only 16 years old when he was one of the 25 best American shooting guards invited to Kobe's camp during the summer. The two shooting guards would form a friendship because of that camp. DeRozan had always tried to emulate and pattern himself after Kobe's game. That was the culmination of his young high school career as one of the Black Mamba's young students.

DeMar DeRozan would use that experience to his advantage. He studied Kobe Bryant even more. He saw how well Bryant used his footwork and pump fakes to get shots up. He learned how to play at the low post by watching how the Mamba operated down there. DeRozan would even try to emulate how Kobe Bryant gets enough space to make the tough shots he has had the habit of making on his way to becoming the third all-time leading scorer in the history of the NBA.[iii]

By the time he was a senior, DeMar DeRozan had become a complete offensive player for Compton High School. He would lead his school to a 26-6 record and a back-to-back championship title in the Moore League. He averaged 29.2 points and eight rebounds as a senior. DeRozan was named a McDonald's All-American in 2008 and was also Moore League MVP. He was also a *Parade* All-American in 2008.

# Chapter 3: College Career

After being considered one of the best high school prospects in the country, having been ranked third by Rivals.com and sixth by Scout.com, DeMar DeRozan had a handful of college programs to choose from after his senior year at Compton High School. The University of California, Los Angeles, was one of the top programs that wanted to secure the services of the high-scoring wing player.

But DeMar DeRozan used the same mentality in choosing his high school as he did in selecting the college program he wanted to attend. He did not want to go to UCLA because, according to his words, everybody goes there. Just like how he decided not to go to Dominguez or transfer to Crossroads, DeMar DeRozan did not want to follow mainstream footsteps. He wanted to do whatever he intended to do. He wanted to start fresh on a team where he could lead and carve his legacy.[iv]

DeRozan's other options for college included Arizona and North Carolina, where two of the best shooting guards in league history, Michael Jordan and Vince Carter, played for college. Nevertheless, he chose to play for the University of Southern California instead of UCLA and the other choices. As his friends and family would say, it was a solid choice that he did not go to UCLA considering how close it was to home and the distractions that came with it. USC was just the proper choice for him.

At USC, DeMar DeRozan continued to pay homage to Kobe Bryant by wearing the superstars' signature Nike sneakers and by choosing to wear the number 10, which was the Mamba's number for Team USA. He would take his Bryant-esque plays with him with the USC Trojans as he tried to carve his legacy of college greatness on his way to making NBA scouts believe in what he could provide for the big leagues.

However, DeMar DeRozan was expected to fill in the huge hole left by another USC alum, who was drafted third overall in the 2008 NBA Draft. OJ Mayo was one of the best high school recruits in school history and was All-Team Pac-10 in his first and only season with the Trojans. He was also responsible for leading USC to the NCAA Tournament. In his first season in the NBA, which was also DeRozan's first season in college, Mayo averaged above 18 points per game. DeMar was expected to make the same impact for the USC Trojans in his freshman season.

The career of DeMar DeRozan with the USC Trojans was projected to go down the same path as OJ Mayo's. He was going to make an impact in his first and only season in college and was going to bolt for the NBA the moment he could. He was also expected to become one of the top prospects in the NBA and a better one than May considering he was bigger and more athletic.

DeMar DeRozan would make his college debut in a win over Azusa Pacific. He immediately showed his quality, scoring 21 points along with seven rebounds in his first game ever as a Trojan. But while DeMar DeRozan struggled with inconsistency in most of his early games, he poured it in when it mattered the most for the USC Trojans.

It was during the Pac-10 Tournament Semifinals when he made it known to one of his final college choices that he meant business with USC. He would finish that win against the UCLA Bruins with 21 points and 13 rebounds. He then had a college career best of 22 points when the USC Trojans won the Pac-10 Finals against Arizona, one of his other choices for college.

But while DeMar DeRozan was named to the All-Freshman Team in the Pac-10 and the tournament MVP, he was a disappointment against better competition, especially in the NCAA Tournament, where USC lost to Michigan State in the second round. He was also considered a disappointment throughout most of his college career, particularly because of his inconsistencies.

DeRozan was one of the top prospects heading into college. Many also considered him a top-five prospect in the Draft once his freshman year was over. But his college numbers were disappointing at best. He was only averaging 13.9 points and 5.7 rebounds despite playing huge minutes. But DeRozan said that people just did not understand that he was still in the process of adjusting to the college game. Despite all that, he was still considered a first-round draft pick despite his stock falling with his subpar college year.

# Chapter 4: NBA Career

## Getting Drafted

DeMar DeRozan declared himself for the 2009 NBA Draft as he had originally planned. He would only play one year with the USC Trojans and jumped straight to the big leagues the first chance he got. He had the size, talent, potential, and work ethic to get into the NBA. He was a sure thing when it came to the draft. The only question was how high he would be drafted.

The 2009 NBA Draft was a comparatively broad class of NBA hopefuls. The consensus top overall pick was Blake Griffin because of how he dominated the college ranks like a man amongst boys. Aside from Griffin, the class would have a total of six future NBA All-Stars. Among those players were future two-time MVP Stephen Curry and perennial MVP contender James Harden. The guard position was also deep in the draft. Curry, Ricky Rubio, and Brandon Jennings were among the top guards in the draft. And with guys like Harden and that year's eventual NBA Rookie of the Year Tyreke Evans, the 2009 NBA Draft had a crop of guards and wing players that DeMar DeRozan had to contend with.

Coming into the draft, DeRozan was considered a lottery pick. He always had good size for the shooting guard position. DeRozan stood nearly 6'7" as a 19-year-old wingman. He had long arms that were measured to be 6'9". He also was not a skinny teenager coming into the NBA. DeMar DeRozan weighed a lean 220 pounds of muscle. He was already a physical specimen despite his youth.

Player comparison was often used by scouts to gauge how far an NBA prospect could get. In DeMar DeRozan's case, he was often compared to Vince Carter. It was not an easy comparison to live up to given the stature and accomplishments that Carter has achieved in his career. But for DeMar, he had the makings of a player just as good, if not better than Carter ever was.

One would not wonder why DeRozan was often compared to Carter. They were the same size. But the parallelism was even closer when it came to raw athletic ability. What made Vince Carter shine as an NBA player was how well he utilized his athletic gifts. He made dunking an art form. Carter would soar through the air to dunk over bigger men or make acrobatic layups. He is often considered the best dunker in NBA history.

DeMar DeRozan was just as good as an athlete coming into the NBA. He had a vertical leap of about 40 inches. He has the prototypical frame of an NBA swingman. He has size, length, speed, quickness, agility, and athleticism for a shooting guard in the big leagues. He is an explosive finisher and high leaper when it came to dunking the ball. When it came to raw athleticism, he had what it took to be the second coming of Vince Carter.

Offensively, DeMar DeRozan knows how to use his athleticism well. He always finds a way to find holes in the defense to get to the basket and finish strong at the rim despite the heavy defensive pressure he was getting from the big men. He has a quick first step when going right. And despite making it known that he will always go right, his first step is quick enough to let him blow past defenders on his way to the basket. And even though DeRozan has a lot of explosiveness and strength to finish at the bucket, he has an array of smooth moves that include floaters and spin moves. [v]

But DeMar DeRozan was more than just a raw athlete that could finish explosively at the basket. He also has a few moves up his sleeves when it came to putting points up on the board. Like his childhood idol Kobe Bryant, DeMar DeRozan loves the midrange game. The perimeter jumper within 20 feet was always DeRozan's bread and butter game, much like how Bryant used that weapon to carve a Hall of Fame career. DeMar floats around the perimeter and knows how to catch and shoot from midrange whenever he gets the ball.[v]

In isolation situations, he has also made it his go-to weapon to dribble the ball once and suddenly rise to shoot a jumper over his defender. With his height and supreme athleticism, he gets a lot of air and space to make his shots from the perimeter. The midrange game, at that point in the NBA, was already a lost art. But DeMar DeRozan had learned to rely on it more than any other prospect did. His offensive game was a fresh reminder of what Michael Jordan and Kobe Bryant could do in their respective primes.

On the other aspects of the game, DeMar DeRozan has consistently proved that he knows how to use his athleticism given that he gets a lot of offensive rebounds when he is near the basket. He has also shown improvement in handling the ball and would also occasionally go out to the college three-point line to show how far he has come with his range.

But while DeMar DeRozan is an athletic freak with the chance of being an offensive force because of his set of attacking moves, he was still a raw prospect at best. He has the potential to become a star in the NBA but his year at USC was not a testament to how much he wanted to be one. DeRozan never looked to dominate back in college despite being the best Trojan on the roster. He often went with the flow and would only show up when he was in the zone.

Inconsistency was often DeMar DeRozan's biggest enemy back in college. There were days when he seemed like a legit future NBA superstar, but he would often float around in other games without making much impact on his team. He has a nice stroke from the floor, but he is still largely inconsistent in his midrange game despite showing flashes of brilliance. He also does not shoot well from the free throw line though the mechanics are already there. The three-point area is also considered a large hole in his game because he rarely takes shots at that distance.[v]

Unlike his idol, DeRozan did not show the killer instinct that made Kobe Bryant one of the best players in the history of the league. He did not show the same passion, intensity, and will to win that Bryant always displays every single night. And also unlike Kobe, he did not go into the post often despite the fact that he has the size and strength to dominate smaller players down low.[v]

In other aspects of the game, DeMar DeRozan seems average at best. He was not a very good ball handler. He did not show the best defensive abilities despite his length and athleticism. And with his height and leaping ability, DeRozan is expected to be a big-time rebounder for the wing position. However, he was also an average player at best when it came to those aspects of the game.

But while he may be a raw prospect, there were many upsides to DeMar DeRozan's game. He had a lot of star potential in himself because of his physical attributes and athleticism. He was not expected to be a good contributor right away, but he was going to be considered as a project player for a team looking to rebuild and be patient in biding their time. And considering that both James Harden and Tyreke Evans had more polished games that DeRozan, it was expected that he was not going to be selected higher than those players.

As the draft day came, expectations came into fruition as Blake Griffin was chosen first overall by the Los Angeles Clippers. The second pick, Hasheem Thabeet, would turn out to be a huge disappointment. Nevertheless, guys like James Harden, who was chosen third overall, proved to be a gem. Fourth overall pick Tyreke Evans would end up winning the Rookie of the Year award. It would take until the ninth pick for DeMar DeRozan's name to get called by the Toronto Raptors. Among the eight players chosen before him, only three ended up developing into All-Stars. Evans was a one-hit wonder. Ricky

Rubio, Jonny Flynn, and Jordan Hill could not live up to their hype. The project, DeMar DeRozan, turned out to be the better pick after all. If one would redraft the class of 2009 all over again, DeRozan would inevitably end up a top-five pick.

## The Rookie Campaign

After having been drafted by the Toronto Raptors, DeMar DeRozan was going to live up to the legacy of the man he was often compared to. Vince Carter started his NBA career as a Raptor back in the late '90s and the early 2000's. He did not make the Toronto Raptors a formidable team in the NBA, but he did give the crowd a show every time he stepped on the court. Carter was flushing down dunk after thunderous dunk every night. That was what DeRozan was expected to do.

DeRozan was also entering a difficult situation with the Toronto Raptors. The established alpha man and star of the team was power forward Chris Bosh. Bosh had been a perennial All-Star in his career with the Raptors. He was known to be one of the top players at his position. But the problem was that he was in the last year of his contract with Toronto. The Raptors had not achieved much since drafting him back in 2003. It was expected that Bosh would bolt out of Toronto the moment he became a free agent.

Despite the impending free agency of their best player, the Toronto Raptors tried their best to surround Chris Bosh with a supporting cast that could convince him to stay. DeMar DeRozan was one of those players expected to lighten the load for the star power forward. Despite being a rookie, he was pushed into the starting shooting guard position while playing alongside either Jose Calderon or Jarrett Jack in the backcourt. One of his roles for the team was to become a buffer that could ease the burden off of Chris Bosh.

DeMar DeRozan would make his NBA debut on October 28, 2009, against the Cleveland Cavaliers led by LeBron James, who was also expected to join the free agency fever after the season. DeRozan would find himself defending the best player in the world during certain situations. While the King may have finished with a triple-double, DeRozan was one of the key players in making him struggle from the field. Meanwhile, the rookie wingman finished the win with eight points and five rebounds in less than 24 minutes of play.

During the early parts of the season, DeRozan would find himself playing inconsistent minutes while also putting up inconsistent single-digit numbers on the board. He would score in double digits for the first time in his career on November 17 against the Denver Nuggets. In that loss, he would make six of nine field goal attempts and score a total of 17 points in a little over 22 minutes of play. It would take eight days for him to score in double digits again. He would go for 12 points in a loss to the Charlotte Hornets.

On December 2, DeMar DeRozan would go for a new career and season high in points. In what became a blowout loss to the Atlanta Hawks, the Raptors focused on giving their long-term project rookie some much-needed exposure and confidence. DeRozan would then respond with his first game of scoring above 20 points. He had 21 points on 6 out of 11 shooting. He attacked the basket relentlessly and finished with a 9 out of 12 shooting clip from the free throw line.

From that point on, DeMar DeRozan found himself in a mini scoring streak. With his confidence at a season high, he would finish the next three games scoring in double digits. He had 16 against the Washington Wizards, 11 versus the Chicago Bulls, and 15 in that game against the Minnesota Timberwolves. All three games were wins for the Toronto Raptors.

One of the more efficient performances that DeMar DeRozan had at that point of the season was when he had 16 points on 6 out of 8 shooting from the field in a big win against the New Jersey Nets on December 18. The Raptors would then win the next four games to finish a five-game winning run. DeRozan had three games of scoring in double digits in those five wins.

It was on January 24, 2010, when DeMar DeRozan would meet his idol on the NBA floor for the first time in his career. Toronto Raptors would host the defending champions the Los Angeles Lakers that night. While DeRozan would try hard to contend with the production that Bryant was putting up, he failed to do so as he still lacked the skill and refinement to keep up with the legendary shooting guard. Bryant would finish the game with 27 points, 16 rebounds, and nine assists. Meanwhile, the Raptors rookie had ten points on 4 out of 12 shooting. But if there was a consolation to that, Toronto ended up with the win.

As a lot of the guards and wing players of the 2009 rookie class were outperforming expectations, DeMar DeRozan was not selected to take part in that season's Rising Stars Challenge during the All-Star Weekend. Nevertheless, he did still participate during the All-Star Weekend as a contestant in the dunk contest. Bringing back the old school style of dunking without props, DeRozan would make it as far as the championship round. However, the 5'9" Nate Robinson would win the fan voting by a mere two percent difference. DeRozan nearly followed the footsteps of Kobe Bryant, who won the contest as a rookie. Vince Carter himself was also a dunk contest champion back in 2000.

The next time that DeMar DeRozan would meet Kobe Bryant was on March 9. This time, the Raptors had home court advantage. It did not matter, though, and the Lakers would win the game. With 32 points, Bryant still owned the inexperienced rookie, who finished the game with only 11 points. After that, DeMar DeRozan would go on a then-personal best of five games of scoring in double digits. His best output during that stretch was when he had 19 points on 7 out of 12 shooting in a win over the Atlanta Hawks on March 17. He played a then season-high of 35 minutes in that game.

In the final game of the regular season for the Toronto Raptors, DeMar DeRozan would go for a new career high in points. In nearly 38 minutes of action, DeRozan was given the reigns over the offense given that the Raptors were already out of playoff contention. He finished the game making 9 of his 11 shots and 6 of his eight free throws to score 24 points. He would also add nine rebounds to his tally in that win against the New York Knicks. Toronto would end the season with 40 wins and 42 losses.

At the conclusion of the season, the raw rookie known as DeMar DeRozan averaged 8.6 points and 2.9 rebounds per game. He shot an all-time career best of 49.8% from the floor given his choice of shot attempts. Nearly 70% of the shots he made during his rookie season were inside the paint. He was making 57.7% of the shots he took near the basket. Those numbers serve as a testament to how well DeRozan was at finishing at the hoop. But at that point, he still needed a lot of work on his perimeter game given how poor he performed in his jump shots.

## The Development Years

During the offseason before the 2010-11 season, the Toronto Raptors' worst expectations came to fruition. Chris Bosh decided to join the free agency market. During the courtship period, he would entertain the idea of playing with superstar guard Dwyane Wade in Miami. Soon, he would commit to playing for the Heat for a discounted price. This prompted LeBron James to follow suit to form a powerhouse trio of him, Bosh, and Wade. This caused a major power surge in the Eastern Conference while thoroughly weakening the Cleveland Cavaliers, and the Toronto Raptors, of course.

Without their franchise player, the Toronto Raptors went into a rebuilding mode. They would focus their offense to big man Andrea Bargnani, who they drafted with the top overall pick a few seasons before. He had been a disappointment since then, but he had his most productive season the moment Chris Bosh left. But the biggest developing story in Toronto was the rise of DeMar DeRozan as their best player and as the new cornerstone of their future as a franchise.

The 21-year-old DeMar DeRozan would take advantage of the situation he was placed in. Given that Bargnani was the team's only other source of offense, DeRozan was given the green light to score as much as he could. It would take only until his third game of the season for him to crack at least 20 points. He would tie his career high in that loss to the Sacramento Kings. He had 24 points on 7 out of 12 shooting from the field. He then had 16 and 15 points respectively in losses to the Utah Jazz and LA Lakers the next two games.

It would not take long for DeMar DeRozan to top his previous career high. On November 12, 2010, in a win over the Orlando Magic, DeRozan would play 40 minutes and would make 8 of his 13 shots and 10 of his 12 free throw attempts to go for a total of 26 points. He also added seven rebounds. Meanwhile, on the other side, the man whose legacy he was following in

Toronto had a mediocre game. Vince Carter only had ten points in that matchup. After that performance, DeRozan would go for 21 in his next game to complete the first time he had back-to-back nights of scoring at least 20 points. The Raptors would lose that game against the powerhouse Miami Heat team.

Come the middle of December, DeMar DeRozan would show how far he got in just a year after underperforming in his rookie season. On December 11, he would start a 14-game streak of scoring in double digits. He began with 16 points in a win over the Detroit Pistons. He would then have 23 points in a loss to the Lakers on December 19. It was during that game when he outscored Kobe for the first time in his career. Bryant only had 20 points as DeRozan slowly narrowed the gap between the two shooting guards.

DeMar DeRozan's best game during that scoring run was when he went for a new career high on December 31 against the Houston Rockets in another loss. He made 12 of his 21 shots and 13 of his 14 free throw attempts to go for a new career best of 37 massive points. He would follow that performance up two days later by going for 27 in a loss to the Boston Celtics.

The next time DeMar DeRozan would taste the sweetness of victory while performing big for the Toronto Raptors was on

January 9 against the Sacramento Kings. He had 28 points on an efficient 13 out of 20 shooting clip during that game. Eight days later, he would go for 23 points in a loss to the New Orleans Hornets before gunning for 28 markers in another loss on January 19.

On January 22, DeRozan would go for his second career game of scoring at least 30 points. He had 30 points on 13 out of 25 shooting from the field in that loss to the Miami Heat. Over the course of the next two games, he had 25 and 29 points respectively against the Memphis Grizzlies and the Philadelphia 76ers. Both games were losses for the Raptors.

Once February started, DeMar DeRozan became a more consistent scorer from the field. Since February up until the end of the season, he would only score below ten points in one game. He had grown to become the most reliable scoring threat for the Toronto Raptors that season as he developed into a future star. During that stretch, he would make the Sophomore Team in the Rising Stars Challenge. He scored 14 points as a starter that night.

One of the highlight moments for DeRozan during the latter parts of the season was when he had 30-point performances in back-to-back games against the New Jersey Nets on March 4 and 5. Then, on March 18, he would go for an efficient 11 out of 15 shooting to score his fifth career 30-point game in that win over the Washington Wizards. Near the end of the season, he had his first double-double performance by finishing that loss to the New York Knicks with 36 points and ten rebounds.

At the end of the season, DeMar DeRozan had grown to become the Toronto Raptors' second-leading scorer and biggest asset for the future. He averaged 17.2 points (double what he had the season before) and 3.8 rebounds. He also shot 46.7% in nearly 35 minutes of action while playing all 82 games for the Toronto Raptors. His free throw shooting clip also improved to 81% that season. Meanwhile, the Raptors were again off to the lottery with their mediocre 22-60 record.

The Toronto Raptors would not make any significant roster changes as the league was headed for a lockout that was induced by a labor dispute between the players' union and the team owners. The only crucial change they made was to hire Dwane Casey as the new head coach that would establish the foundations of what would soon become a strong defensive team.

The season would be shortened to 66 games and would start late in December. This caused certain players to slack off in their training. Training camp was also compressed to the point that teams were not able to mesh well with one another. But the season had to start nonetheless. In the Raptors' season debut on December 26, DeMar DeRozan would go for 15 points in a win over the Cleveland Cavaliers.

DeMar DeRozan would proceed to score in double digits in all of his first six games. He scored at least 20 points in three of those outings. The best one was when he had 25 points on 9 out of 18 shooting against the Cleveland Cavaliers on January 4, 2012. The Raptors were a healthy 3-3 at that early point of the compressed season.

The worst would come for the Toronto Raptors as Andrea Bargnani, their leading scorer the past two seasons, went down with an injury in the middle of January. This forced DeMar DeRozan to carry more load on the offense. While one would usually think that this was a moment for DeRozan to strut his stuff as the primary scorer for the Raptors, Bargnani's injury worked to his disadvantage.

With no other scoring threat on the Raptors' lineup, defenses were focusing on DeMar DeRozan from that point on. He was getting doubled or even tripled out on the perimeter. Paint defenders would collapse on him whenever he got near the basket. This caused DeRozan to shoot poorly from the field in the first 11 games since losing Bargnani. He would shoot above 50% from the field in only three of those 11 games. He even shot below 30% four times since losing Bargnani in that span of games.

Nevertheless, DeRozan would find some semblance of consistency come the month of February. While there were still nights wherein he would shoot dreadfully from the field, he had redeeming performances as well. He would have 25 points in a loss to the Miami Heat on February 5, 2012. Then, three days later, he would have the same amount of points in a loss to the Milwaukee Bucks before going for 21 in a win over the Boston Celtics on February 10.

On February 15, DeMar DeRozan went for a then-season high of 29 points on 13 out of 21 shooting from the field in a loss to the San Antonio Spurs. He followed that up by scoring 24 in a loss to the Charlotte Bobcats two days later and then 23 points in a win over the Detroit Pistons on February 22. He also added seven rebounds in that win over Detroit.

Bargnani's return to the lineup in March helped DeMar DeRozan play a lot better without the versatile 7-footer. With defenses giving him the normal looks he used to have before losing the Italian center to injury, DeRozan would go 20 consecutive games of scoring in double digits from March until the final few games of the regular season.

Some of the highlights included his season high of 30 points on 11 out of 17 shooting in a win against the New York Knicks on March 23. A week after that, he had 28 points in a loss to the Miami Heat. DeRozan would get another 28-point performance on April 6 when the Raptors lost to the Cavs. Overall during that streak, DeMar DeRozan scored at least 20 points in nine out of the 20 games.

The end of the regular season DeMar DeRozan would average 16.7 points and 3.3 rebounds. His scoring and his field goal percentage of 42.2% saw a dip because of the struggles he faced when Bargnani was out with an injury. The Raptors were not also doing well having won only 23 of the 66 games they played. For the third time since getting drafted, DeMar DeRozan was yet to see playoff action.

## Teaming Up with Kyle Lowry, the Rudy Gay Experiment

The Toronto Raptors would work hard to shake the roster up a little bit coming into the 2012-13 season. They would retain their core but would also bring in Kyle Lowry, who was traded from the Houston Rockets during the offseason. While point guard Jose Calderon was a quality playmaker and shooter, Lowry brought in feisty defense and top-level leadership qualities at the point guard position. They also fielded two new productive rookies who they drafted with their last two first-round picks. Big man Jonas Valanciunas was drafted back in 2011 while wing player Terrence Ross was drafted eighth overall in 2012.

The 2012-13 season would also mark the year when DeMar DeRozan would become the leading man for the Toronto Raptors. He was the top option for offense and points. As seen from his start, the Raptors did indeed believe that their young wingman had the makings of a great shooting guard in the league. He would open his first five games scoring at least 20 points in three games.

It would also not take long for him to tie his career best. On November 12, 2012, DeMar DeRozan would make 16 of his 33 shots from the field in a loss to the Utah Jazz. He would finish with 37 points, eight rebounds, and six assists, which was an impressive number for him given that DeRozan was never much of a playmaker. But unfortunately for the Toronto Raptors, they would only win four out of the first 20 games that they played early in that season.

When Andrea Bargnani again went down with an injury in December, the Toronto Raptors would fare better than they ever did with him in the lineup. Guys like Amir Johnson, Ed Davis, and young rookie center Jonas Valanciunas would step up big to help DeRozan and Lowry specifically on the defensive end of the floor. After Bargnani went down, the Raptors would have a winning record for December. During that month, DeRozan had his only game of scoring below ten points. His best output was when he had 30 points in a win over the New Orleans Hornets on December 28.

DeMar DeRozan was also doing well during January of 2013. He would only have three games wherein he scored less than ten points. He was even becoming more of a playmaker as he had three games of dishing out seven or more assists during that month. It was also at the end of the month when the Toronto Raptors announced a roster shakeup.

The Toronto Raptors would finalize a deal that would send Jose Calderon and Ed Davis over to the Memphis Grizzlies in exchange for high-flying and high-scoring small forward Rudy Gay. Gay was a similar player to DeRozan. He was an athletic wing that played above the rim. He also had a penchant for playing isolation basketball and for going for midrange jumpers. He was an older version of DeMar DeRozan. The acquisition of

Gay gave the Raptors a pair of high-flying players waiting in the wings.

The Rudy Gay experiment initially worked. DeRozan and Gay would form a duo that ran gave wing defenders nightmares. While both players needed the ball to be effective, DeRozan found himself becoming more efficient because of the lighter defensive looks he was seeing. He had seven games of scoring above 20 points during the month of February since the Raptors acquired Gay. It was on February 27 when he even went for 34 points on 10 out of 19 shooting from the field in a loss to the Cleveland Cavaliers. He made 14 of his 15 free throws that game. Toronto would also win seven of their 12 games that month.

DeRozan's growth as a player was even more evident given that, in the final 24 games of the season, he would only have two games where he failed to score in double digits. He had become a model of consistency on the scoring end. He even had back-to-back 30-point games near the end of the season. He had 36 points against the Brooklyn Nets on April 14 before going for 30 markers two days later versus the Atlanta Hawks. Both games were wins, and the Toronto Raptors were in the middle of a five-game winning streak in their quest for a playoff spot.

Having played all 82 games of the season, DeMar DeRozan would average a new career high of 18.1 points together with 3.9 rebounds and 2.5 assists. The Toronto Raptors were also improving as their future star wingman was rising. They won 34 out of the 82 games they played that season. It was a marked improvement from the previous years since losing Chris Bosh to the Miami Heat in 2010.

## First All-Star Season, Playoff Debut

The 2013-14 season would be a defining one not only for DeMar DeRozan but the entire Toronto Raptors team as well. Valanciunas developed into a solid center for the team. Terrence Ross was a good option off the bench. Kyle Lowry became one of the better starting point guards in the league. But the biggest transformation was DeRozan, who embraced his role as the team's best offensive weapon.

It would not take time for DeMar DeRozan to explode offensively. In his second game, which was a loss to the Atlanta Hawks, he would go for 31 points on 14 out of 23 shooting from the field. But again, there were initial problems that the Raptors had to resolve. Both Rudy Gay and DeMar DeRozan initially struggled to play alongside each other that season because both played the same style. The difference was that DeRozan moved well without the ball while Gay needed the ball. Worse, he had a huge sum on his name. His contract that time was among the biggest in the NBA. The Raptors needed to let him go and move on to greener pastures.

Nineteen games into the season, the Toronto Raptors would break apart their duo of high-scoring and high-flying wingmen by trading away Rudy Gay to the Sacramento Kings for a package that included productive role players and scorers. The move was seen as a financial decision as it allowed the Raptors to shell off Gay's massive contract. It also allowed DeMar DeRozan to have room to grow on the offensive end as the unquestioned go-to guy.

After the trade, DeMar DeRozan only became a more potent threat on the offensive end. He would constantly figure himself as a double-digit scorer with performances above 20 points or more. He had his fourth game of scoring at least 30 points as early as December 18 when the Raptors lost to the Charlotte Bobcats. During December alone, he had six games of scoring over 20 points.

DeMar DeRozan only got better and better as the season unfolded. In January 2014, he was consistently scoring above 20 points. He had ten of those that month alone. Those games included one where he put up a new career high in points. It was on January 22, 2014, when DeMar DeRozan made 15 of his 22 shots and 9 of his 14 free throws to go for a total of 40 points in a win over the Dallas Mavericks. The following game, he retained his hot hand when he finished a win over the Philadelphia 76ers with 34 points and nine rebounds.

He was just as productive in the month of February. On February 1, he would go for a double-double game of 36 points and 12 assists in a loss to the Portland Trailblazers. Then, barely a week later in a loss to the LA Clippers, he finished with 36 points and eight assists. And in his final game before the All-Star break, he had 31 points in a win against the Atlanta Hawks.

By the middle of February, All-Star Weekend got going, and DeMar DeRozan was on his way to it, but not as a Rising Stars Challenge competitor nor as a Dunk Contest contestant. He was selected as one of the reserves for the Eastern All-Stars. He did not disappoint in his first All-Star Game after scoring 8 points in 14 minutes of action for the winning East team.

Shortly after the midseason break, DeMar DeRozan continued to show his class as a rising star in the league. He had back-to-back-to-back games of scoring at least 30 points at the end of the month. He had 33 points in a win over the Cavs on February

25 before going for 34 points against the Wizards in a loss in a triple-overtime classic. He ended the run with 32 points in a win over the Golden State Warriors on March 2.

From that point on, DeMar DeRozan had solidified his name as one of the premier shooting guards in the league. In his final 21 games for the season, he scored at least 20 points 14 times. Four of those occasions were games where he had at least 30 points. He had finally grown into his potential as a formidable star in a league that needed production from the wing position.

At the end of the season, DeMar DeRozan averaged then-career highs of 22.7 points, 4.3 rebounds, and 4.0 assists. He played 79 games for the season while averaging 38 minutes every night. His backcourt mate Kyle Lowry also did well after putting up stats worthy of an All-Star berth. However, he was one of the biggest snubs in that event. DeRozan and Lowry would lead the Raptors to a 48-34 record, which helped them clinch a playoff spot for the first time since the days of Chris Bosh. Those 48 wins were a franchise record for the Toronto Raptors. No other Raptor had led the team to such an accomplishment including Vince Carter or Chris Bosh. It was DeMar DeRozan that did it.

DeMar DeRozan would make his playoff debut against a Brooklyn Nets team that fielded a group of old All-Stars that were already in the twilight years of their respective careers. It was the Raptors' youth against the experience and wisdom of the Nets' Paul Pierce, Kevin Garnett, and Joe Johnson, among others. The Raptors may have had the fresher legs, but the Nets had been playing that game longer than they had.

DeRozan did not have the best playoff debut for any young star. The stifling defense that the Nets played on him in Game 1 and the playoff jitters that came with his debut would only allow him to make 3 of his 13 baskets. DeMar DeRozan would only score 14 points in Game 1 as the Brooklyn Nets drew first blood.

Come Game 2, DeMar DeRozan would shake off the jitters and tough defense to dominate on the offensive end. He relentlessly attacked the basket to make 9 of his 21 shots and 12 of his 14 free throws to score a total of 30 points in a win for the Toronto Raptors over the Brooklyn Nets in Game 1 to tie the series up with one win apiece.

While DeMar DeRozan was just as good as he was in Game 2 during Game 3, the Toronto Raptors badly needed help from all around the floor as the All-Star wingman was the only bright spot for the team. Though DeRozan would make 8 of his 22 shots and 13 of his 15 free throws to score 30 points for the second straight game, the Nets had more weapons that contributed on the offense to take back the series lead. As a consolation, DeMar DeRozan became the first Raptor since Vince Carter to score 30 points in consecutive playoff games.

In Game 4, DeRozan's backcourt mate Kyle Lowry would step up big time to help the team's leading scorer in their quest to push the series even longer. Lowry would have 22 points in addition to the efforts put up by role players such as Amir Johnson, Greivis Vasquez, and Patrick Patterson to help the Toronto Raptors tie the series once more. DeRozan, on a terrible 7 out of 19 shooting night, would finish the game with 24 points.

Back in Toronto for Game 5, the Raptors would again see their other role players stepping up big to assist the backcourt duo of DeRozan and Lowry. Johnson, Valanciunas, and Vasquez all scored in double digits. DeRozan, who lived from the free throw line yet again, finished the game with 23 points. But the main story was Kyle Lowry, who had 36 points while making 6 of his nine three-point attempts that game to give the Toronto Raptors the series lead for the first time.

Though they were one game away from heading into the second round of the playoffs, things quickly normalized again for the Toronto Raptors. DeMar DeRozan remained the only consistent bright spot for the team after two games of seeing help from the role players. He would score 28 points on 8 out of 18 shooting from the field. The only other guy who scored in double digits was Kyle Lowry, who had 11 points on a terrible shooting night. The Nets were able to push the series to Game 7 after that win in Game 6.

In Game 7, everyone on the team tried to step up to the plate to challenge the Brooklyn Nets in their quest to seek a second round appearance. The starters and certain role players were clicking from the floor. Johnson, Ross, and Patterson were doing well in helping the Raptors' star backcourt duo. However, the Nets were playing just as well and the game was a near stalemate. In the end, experience won out as Brooklyn took home the win by a mere point. DeMar DeRozan would not have the best game of the series with only 18 points, though he averaged 23.9 points during the seven-game run. Lowry finished with 28 points.

Despite the fact that the Toronto Raptors' playoff run ended quickly in the first round of the 2014 playoffs, there were some positives to take from what was arguably the franchise's best season. They had won a franchise-best of 48 wins. DeMar DeRozan had developed into a quality All-Star and scorer for a team still looking to improve. Kyle Lowry was also growing well into his own as one of the better starting point guards in the league. Young role players such as Jonas Valanciunas and Terrence Ross were also stepping up in certain situations.

Speaking of Ross, there was a buzz that Toronto had found its new Tracy McGrady to DeMar DeRozan's Vince Carter. Back in the days when Carter was still flying high in Toronto, the Toronto Raptors also had a capable wingman backing him up from the bench. Tracy McGrady, who was selected straight out of high school during the 1997 NBA Draft, was one of the best prep players in recent memory. However, it took him some time to adjust to the NBA game since high school was a different story.

While McGrady was still taking his time, Carter came in 1998 and immediately gave a positive impact to the Raptors as his college experience helped him prepare for the NBA better than McGrady. Unknown to the two wingmen, they were distant cousins. Though there were hardly any rifts between Carter and McGrady, everybody knew how much potential and talent the latter had once he finally grew into himself. But Tracy McGrady could not flourish in Toronto because Vince Carter was the established alpha. It was not until he moved to the Orlando Magic a few seasons later when he established himself as a real superstar.

Fans were starting to believe that they were seeing the same kind of tandem in that season's Toronto Raptors. DeMar DeRozan was the proven alpha and primary scorer for the Raptors at that point of his career. However, Terrence Ross, who was in the second year of his career in the NBA, showed just as much promise. He was a freakish athlete that probably had better hops than DeRozan. He was a better three-point shooter than his more established teammate. He had the makings of a star but was not quite there yet, just as McGrady was when Carter was the established alpha in the locker room.

It was not until Ross put up 51 points against the Los Angeles Clippers sometime in January when people began to see that he had the makings of a star. Those 51 points were mostly scored from the perimeter as the sophomore guard was outplaying even DeMar DeRozan that game, who could not score 51 points on any given night. But while Ross's outburst in that game was impressive, DeRozan remained the more consistent out of the two. Ross would never have the same type of performance the entire year while DeRozan was putting up consistent All-Star numbers. Whether he would become the next Tracy McGrady was still a question left unanswered. Meanwhile, DeMar DeRozan had already established himself as a player ready to challenge Vince Carter's legacy in Toronto.

For DeRozan's part, his growth that season was mainly noticeable as far as his other NBA peers were concerned. It was not only within the team that his development was evident. The whole NBA landscape saw how far DeMar had gone since getting drafted as a project player back in 2009. Almost nobody could predict that he would get as far as he did that season.

In 2012, he was rewarded with a hefty contract extension by the Toronto Raptors, who believed that he would become the face of the franchise years later, though he was yet to take them close to the playoffs or even make an All-Star team at that point in his career. The contract only gave him more attention, but DeRozan never changed his approach to the game. He was biding his time and doing things he was used to doing.[vi]

One of DeRozan's childhood friends that grew up with him near Los Angeles, James Harden, was equally in awe at how far the Raptors star had reached. He believed that though DeRozan never changed his approach and style, he was more focused on getting out there to perform rather than looking at the little things that caused distractions. He was even prouder that DeRozan was one of the players he was playing alongside in the Team USA training camp.

Indiana Pacers star Paul George had a similar journey. Nobody saw him as a player that could dominate the floor. He was drafted as the tenth pick of the 2010 NBA Draft but took his time to develop into a star. Whenever DeRozan and George played opposite each other, the Raptors star always had kind words when talking about how far George has jumped from being a role player to a legitimate two-way star.

This time, it was Paul George who had kind words for DeRozan. The two stars knew each other from high school and had clashed on the hard floor several times in the past. George saw how far DeRozan jumped from being a raw prospect to an All-Star that could lead a team to the playoffs. He marveled at how DeMar would add new moves and facets to his offensive game every year. He knew that the Raptors star takes his game and role with a serious approach.[vi] DeRozan wanted to get better every year.

John Wall, the Washington Wizards' star point guard who also saw the playoffs for the first time that season, had praises for DeRozan's growth. He had known the wingman since they were young. Their relationship only improved because of the Team USA training camp. He knew how great of a player and an even better person DeRozan was because of the bond they have shared as best friends. John Wall knew that his friend had an inner drive to become a much better player. A mere postseason appearance was not enough for him.

## Injury Struggles, Lowry's Evolution into an All-Star

During the offseason, DeMar DeRozan kept to mind that loss to the Brooklyn Nets in Game 7. Had he scored one more point, things would have been different. Had he drained one more shot, the Raptors would have won. Keeping that in mind, he improved his game even further heading into another season where the Raptors were expected to toil towards the postseason again.

DeMar DeRozan would take the time to train with legendary center Hakeem Olajuwon. Olajuwon is regarded as one of the best centers in league history. Nobody in the history of the game had more moves down at the low post. DeRozan wanted to learn from the best, just like how Kobe perfected his post moves by training with Hakeem several years back. He was trying to elevate his game to new heights.[vi]

After training with Olajuwon, DeMar DeRozan then focused on improving his handles. He knew he could become a more dangerous player by developing his left hand. Everybody knew he was always going to the right. Developing his left-hand handles would help him develop a new side to his game. He would start doing routine tasks with his left hand. DeRozan accustomed himself to writing and eating with his non-dominant hand. Other than that, he also hired ball handling experts to help him train his handles. He was trying to become a complete basketball player.[vi]

The Toronto Raptors, on their part, retained the same core of players that got them to a franchise-best record the previous season. The only key addition they made was bringing in combo guard Lou Williams, who always had a knack for scoring big off the bench, to reinforce the Raptors' group of backup players. The core of the team still revolved around DeRozan and Lowry.

DeMar DeRozan immediately made noise the moment he made his 2014-15 season debut. In that win against the Atlanta Hawks, he would go for 15 points and career highs of 11 rebounds and six steals. Always known as a one-dimensional player that relied more on his offensive game rather than the other aspects of basketball, DeMar DeRozan showed flashes of what he could become if he made an effort on the other end of the court.

At the early parts of the season, it seemed like DeMar DeRozan was still feeling the high of getting named an All-Star for the first time in his career last season. He was putting up All-Star numbers. In his first 15 games of the season, he scored above 20 points in ten of those outings. His then-season high was 30 points, which he scored in a loss to the Miami Heat on November 2, 2014. He made 11 of his 22 field goals that night. In other games, he was consistently figuring himself in the mid-20's concerning scoring output.

But after a struggle on November 28 in a loss to the Dallas Mavericks, it was clear that DeMar DeRozan had suffered an injury after playing only 20 minutes and scoring zero points. A day later, he was ruled out indefinitely because of a torn tendon in his left leg's adductor. The injury happened during the third quarter of that game against the Mavericks. After leaving that game, he did not return.

DeMar DeRozan missed 21 consecutive games while trying to rehabilitate and recover from that injury. During his absence, the Toronto Raptors tried to stay afloat by relying more on Kyle Lowry and bench scorer Lou Williams among other role players that stepped up to the challenge of filling the hole left by DeRozan. The Raptors would win 12 of those 21 games that DeRozan missed.

The All-Star wingman would make his return on January 14, 2015, against the Philadelphia 76ers. In only about 29 minutes of play, DeMar DeRozan looked like he did not miss significant time on the court after making 9 of his 14 shots to score 20 points. Over the course of the next two games, he would score 25 against Atlanta and 22 versus the New Orleans Pelicans. The Raptors would lose both games. DeRozan would see a slight slump in the next three games after those performances. He would combine for only a 14 points in those three outings.

Nevertheless, DeMar DeRozan would spring back to form by scoring 25 points in a win over the Detroit Pistons. After that, he had 24 in a win against the Indiana Pacers on January 27. He finished January high by going for a near triple-double effort. In a win versus the Washington Wizards, DeMar DeRozan finished with 15 points, ten rebounds, and seven assists.

When the All-Star Weekend got rolling, DeMar DeRozan was not among the players selected to play for the East in the midseason classic. Instead, the Raptor chosen as an All-Star was Kyle Lowry, who was going to play in his first ever All-Star Game. The evolution of Lowry as an All-Star effectively gave the Toronto Raptors the franchise's first duo of All-Stars.

Shortly after the midseason break, DeMar DeRozan would go for a season high in points on March 2. In that win over the Sixers, he made 12 of his 24 shots and all 10 of his free throws to score a total of 35 points. He also added nine rebounds and five assists in the process. Over the course of the next four games, he scored at least 20 points consecutively. Those games included a 30-point performance against the Cleveland Cavaliers.

On March 30, DeMar DeRozan would have the best game of his professional career at that point. In a win over the Houston Rockets, it was a matchup between the two best young shooting guards in the league. It was James Harden on one end while DeRozan was on the other. The Raptor guard would outplay his counterpart the entire game after making 14 of his 27 field goals and 12 of his 17 free throws for a career high of 42 points. In addition to that, he also had 11 rebounds to outplay Harden, who had 31 points.

Before the season ended, DeMar DeRozan would pour in another high-scoring game by going for 38 points in a loss to the Boston Celtics on April 4. He made 14 of his 25 field goals and 10 of his 12 free throws in that game. Had DeRozan not missed consecutive games and had he not been hampered because of the injury, he would have surely been an All-Star as seen from the numbers he was putting up in the latter part of the season.

At the end of the regular season, DeMar DeRozan averaged 20.1 points, 4.6 rebounds, and 3.5 assists. His backcourt mate was scoring nearly 18 points a night and was the team's best player during his prolonged absence. Like the previous year, the Raptors would again reset the franchise record for wins. This time, they won 49 games heading into another postseason appearance.

The Toronto Raptors would meet the Washington Wizards in the first round of the playoffs. While it would seem that the matchup was equal on paper, the results were utterly embarrassing for the Raptors. It was going to end up as a four-game sweep for the Wizards, who were not even one of the more dominant teams in the East.

In Game 1, DeRozan struggled against a tight defense that forced him to shoot a terrible clip of 6 out of 20 from the floor. He ended up with 15 points, 11 rebounds, and six assists in that game. In the next game, he would have a much better shooting performance, but the Raptors were widely inconsistent to keep up with the Wizards. DeRozan had 20 points and seven assists in that game.

Game 3 was his best playoff performance. DeMar DeRozan would break a franchise record for points in the first quarter by going for 20 in the opening period. The man he surpassed was Vince Carter, who had 19. While he may have been hot the first 12 minutes, defenses keyed in on him while other Raptors were struggling to contribute. DeRozan's hot shooting cooled down, and he ended up with 32 points that night in another loss. In the next game, the Wizards demolished them by 31 big points to complete a four-game sweep of the first round.

The Toronto Raptors' first-round fiasco was embarrassing. They had the makings of a second round team, but struggled against a team that was not much better than they were. Fingers pointed to the inconsistencies in the Raptors' role players and how they could not match the intensity and production of DeMar DeRozan. People were even blaming Kyle Lowry, whose performance saw a significant drop after the midway point of the season. That performance signified to the front office that changes were needed as far as the complementary players were concerned.

## Breaking Through to the Conference Finals

Significant changes and additions were made during the offseason before the 2015-16 season. The Toronto Raptors added a legitimate small forward in DeMarre Carroll after years of toiling with Terrence Ross as the starter in that position. They then acquired veteran versatile power forward, Luis Scola, to bring in some toughness at the frontcourt. Cory Joseph and Bismack Biyombo were also significant upgrades as backups for the point guard and center positions respectively.

But the best thing that happened to the Raptors during the offseason, other than the additions of new key players and DeRozan's continued development, was Kyle Lowry's transformation. From being a pudgy and slow point guard that often got winded early, Lowry underwent a total body metamorphosis and shed a lot of weight and fat. He was leaner and healthier coming into the new season.

With better supporting players around him, DeMar DeRozan would lead the Toronto Raptors to a strong start to the season. He would help his team open the season with a 5-0 record. He had four games of scoring above 20 points in those five wins. His best was when he had 28 points on 7 out of 18 shooting from the floor and 14 out of 15 from the field in a win over the Oklahoma City Thunder on November 4.

On November 15, DeRozan would show a developing playmaker side to his game after going for a double-double of 15 points and 11 assists in a win against the New Orleans Pelicans. Two days later, it was his defense that was on display after finishing a loss to the Sacramento Kings with 24 points and five steals. This was the season when DeMar DeRozan was trying to climb his way back to stardom by doing everything else on the floor better than he had in his career.

But something significant transpired that season. It was not something related to DeMar DeRozan directly, but it was an event that culminated a basketball fan's worship of a legend that started in 1996. Late in November 2015, shooting guard legend Kobe Bryant announced that he was leaving basketball for good because of a combination of injuries that left him unable to compete at the highest level. He still loved basketball, but his body could not take it. This was the man that DeMar DeRozan had idolized since he was a young boy growing up in Compton.

Without Kobe Bryant, DeMar DeRozan would not have been the star player he was at that point of his career. Sure, DeRozan is an athletic freak and has size to boot. But watching and learning from Bryant got him to where he is. The Black Mamba was always his favorite player as a child and even as an NBA professional.

Growing up in Compton near Los Angeles, DeMar DeRozan closely monitored Kobe Bryant's career. From the air balls in 1997 to the three-peat with Shaquille O'Neal in the early 2000's, the MVP, and two other titles he won late in the decade, DeRozan had seen it all. He followed Bryant's work ethic. Kobe was never the most athletic nor the most talented. But he made up for it with sheer hard work, passion, and dedication to his craft to the point that it was maniacal. That was what rubbed off on players like DeMar DeRozan.

DeRozan would follow Kobe's moves and try to perfect them on his own. He emulated Bryant's game. He honed the midrange game, which was always Kobe's favorite shot. He studied every move that the Mamba had in his bag of tricks. From pump fakes to crossover moves and pivot masteries, DeRozan tried it all and had seen success with them.

The friendship that used to be mere admiration started when DeMar DeRozan was only 16 years old and was invited to Kobe's camp. From then on, he and Bryant began a relationship that continued until DeRozan made the NBA. Despite being on equal footing as far as being professionals were concerned, DeRozan was always intimidated and in awe of Bryant whenever they met face-to-face. But he never backed down. Every time they saw each other on the hard floor, they duked it out. Kobe would not take it easy on the youngster, and the youngster took it to the legend. And every time after they met, DeRozan was left with more experience and material to work on.

As DeMar DeRozan's NBA career continued, he was looking more like Kobe every year. Aside from wearing Bryant's signature sneaker line, DeRozan honed his midrange game to perfection. It was always Kobe's biggest weapon. DeMar never relied too much on the three-point area since Bryant did not dwell too much outside, though he once held the record for most three-pointers made in a game (12 three-pointers, which were later broken by Stephen Curry, who had 13).

And at this point in DeRozan's career, he also worked on his post game. He played more with his back to the basket, especially against smaller defenders, much like how Kobe Bryant did. He tried every trick in the book like drop steps, sidesteps, and turnaround jumpers. And while DeRozan never relied on the three-pointer much like Bryant did, he tried to make for it by attacking the basket and getting fouled often like his idol. He was not afraid to challenge the rim protectors and get contact. He was Kobe Bryant Part Two out there on the court.

With Kobe Bryant retiring, DeMar DeRozan was one of the players left to take on his mantle. In the NBA today, he is the closest thing to Bryant as far as style and talents are concerned. Most shooting guards dwell outside the perimeter to shoot three-pointers. Some of them are more like combo guards that could play the point guard and shooting guard positions well. But DeRozan was the only player in the league that tried to be Kobe Bryant until he became his own person. But at that point in his career, DeRozan was trying to become more like Kobe by winning. He may be looking forward to the final few games he got to match up with the Mamba, but his focus was a ring.

As the season went on, DeMar DeRozan would score a new season high of 34 points together with five rebounds and five assists in a loss to the Denver Nuggets on December 3. He was 14 out of 26 from the field in that game. At that point of the season, the Raptors were a healthy 12-8 throughout their first 20 games. They were on pace to break their franchise record once again.

Shortly after that, DeRozan would have a marvelous week for the Toronto Raptors. From December 7 to 13, he was named the Eastern Conference Player of the Week for the first time in his career. He averaged 24 points in the four games he played that week while the Raptors went undefeated.

It was on that December 7 game when DeMar DeRozan would face Kobe Bryant on the hard floor for the final time in his career. The Raptors would host the Lakers that night. DeRozan, unfortunately, was probably too awestruck and teary-eyed to make noise in his final matchup versus the Mamba. Kobe would outscore him by putting up 21 points. Meanwhile, DeMar DeRozan had 16 points, five rebounds, and six assists. While Toronto got the win, the important aspect of that game was the memories that DeRozan got from facing his idol for the final time.

Proceeding on, DeRozan would go for at least 30 points for the second and third time that season. On December 17, he had 31 points on 12 out of 25 shooting from the field in a loss to the Charlotte Hornets. After that, he went for 30 points by shooting 10 out of 17 from the floor in a win against the Miami Heat. DcMar would end the year right by going for 34 points in a win over the Washington Wizards on December 30. He was 9 out of 24 from the floor and 15 out of 15 from the free-throw line in that game.

DeMar DeRozan would have an unbelievable month of January. It started when he had a new season high of 35 points in a win over the Wizards on January 8. He was 11 out of 24 from the field and 12 out of 13 from the free-throw line in that game. He also added eight rebounds.

Then, on January 18, he had a three-game streak of scoring at least 30 points. He would go for 30 against the Brooklyn Nets before dominating the Boston Celtics with 34 points and six rebounds. Then, on January 22, he would go for 33 points, six rebounds, and four assists against the Miami Heat in a 20-point win. The Raptors would win all three of those games.

At the end of January, the Toronto Raptors were the league's hottest group of contenders. They would only lose two out of the 14 games they played that season. That included a franchise best of 11 consecutive games without a loss. Because of such a feat, both DeMar DeRozan and Kyle Lowry were named the Eastern Conference Players of the Month.

DeMar DeRozan was again named an NBA All-Star for February. He and Kyle Lowry were the first backcourt mates in franchise history to be chosen as All-Stars in the same season. This was DeRozan's second time to be named as an All-Star in his seven-year NBA career. And it was not going to be the last one as he was yet to reach the prime of his career.

On March 4, DeMar DeRozan would go for a new season-high 38 points in a win against the Portland Trailblazers. Though he would only go for 7 out of 19 from the floor in that game, what got him to 38 points was the number of foul shots he was given. DeRozan relentlessly attacked the basket to seek contact. The result was that he was given 25 charity shots, and he drained 24 of them.

Eight days later, DeMar DeRozan would equal that scoring total but had a better all-around performance in that win against the Miami Heat. Aside from the 38 points he scored on a 13 out of 26 shooting clip, he also had ten rebounds and seven assists to nearly capture what would have been his first career triple-double. He was showing how improved of an all-around player he was at that point of his career.

At the end of the regular season, DeMar DeRozan averaged a new career high of 23.5 points on top of the 4.5 rebounds and 4.0 assists he was getting each night. More importantly, his shooting percentage improved to 44.6% despite taking more shots that season. DeRozan also averaged a then-career best of 85% from the line as he showed a lot of improvement and refinement in his offensive game. He also moved up to second place behind Chris Bosh on the list of the franchise's best scorers. He would push the Toronto Raptors to a franchise-best record of 56 wins. They were the second seed in an increasingly competitive Eastern Conference.

The playoffs did not start well for DeMar DeRozan. It was a matchup against the Indiana Pacers in the first round. Going up against Paul George, who was also an avid fan of Bryant, DeRozan could not get a shot up against one of the best defenders in the league at the time. He would finish with only 14 points on a 26% shooting clip from the floor. The Raptors would lose their home court advantage with that loss.

Game 2 was the same story for DeRozan. Against the stifling perimeter defense of the bigger and longer Paul George, DeRozan would shoot 5 out of 18 from the floor to finish the game with 10 points. However, everyone else on the roster stepped up to score a win for the Raptors. The series was tied 1-1 even though DeRozan was not in best form.

While DeMar DeRozan would still struggle shooting from the field in Game 3, he did enough damage from the free throw line to go for a total of 21 points in addition to helping his team get the win and their home court advantage back. Unfortunately, the Pacers dug deep and kept the defense focused on DeRozan, who only had eight points in what was an embarrassing performance for him.

But DeMar DeRozan would bounce back quickly. In Game 5, he would shoot well from the field while getting fouled several times. He shot 10 out of 22 from the floor and 12 out of 13 from the free throw line to record a then-playoff best of 34 points.

More importantly, his team needed his production as the Raptors barely won that game.

Come Game 6, DeMar DeRozan would fall to earth after being on Cloud Nine in Game 5. He was limited to 3 out of 13 from the field and only 8 points as the Indiana Pacers blew them out to force a do-or-die Game 7. In Game 7, DeRozan did not care whether he was missing or making his shots. He was chucking up shots similar to how Kobe Bryant did. He would shoot a total of 32 shots from the floor while making only ten of them. Nevertheless, he ended up with 30 points and the crucial win to proceed to the next round for the first time in his career.

The Toronto Raptors would again face another tough challenge in the second round of the playoffs. It was in the form of the Miami Heat led by another all-time great shooting guard, Dwyane Wade. The Heat and Wade would immediately make their presence felt by robbing the Toronto Raptors of their home court advantage in Game 1. While DeRozan did not feel the same defensive pressure that he felt against Paul George, he still could not do enough to win that opening bout. He finished the game with 22 points on 9 out of 22 shooting.

Come Game 2, DeMar DeRozan still did not have the best outing, but he remained as gritty as his team to prevent a 0-2 hole. He would end the game with 20 points on 9 out of 24 shooting from the floor and along with eight rebounds. He also added three steals to his name in that match. Then, in Game 3, he and the Raptors regained home-court advantage by stealing one in Miami. He had 19 points, six rebounds, and five assists. DeRozan shot another poor percentage from the field in that game.

Game 4 would end up being his worst playoff game of that series. DeMar DeRozan was shooting blanks from the floor and was not even attacking the basket like he was expected to do. He was 4 out of 17 from the field and ended up with only nine points in a loss that tied the series up 2-2. The rest of the series would end up a best-of-three just like in the first round.

Not willing to give up the series lead, DeMar DeRozan would explode in Game 5 as the series went back to Toronto. He tied his playoff high with 34 points on an 11 out of 22 shooting clip. He also made all 11 of his free throws in that game. DeRozan's production in only 34 minutes of play helped the Toronto Raptors regain the series lead and were one game away from reaching the Conference Finals.

Despite the fact that DeRozan would have a decent outing in Game 6, the Miami Heat would go on to force Game 7 on the

Toronto Raptors, who were in the middle of another full seven-game series. DeMar had 23 points in that match. Forcing Game 7 might have exhausted the Miami Heat as they would end up losing the bout by a huge margin. DeMar DeRozan may have contributed 28 points to that win, but it was largely a team effort as the Raptors won the game by 27 points.

Winning Game 7 against the Miami Heat in the second round catapulted the Toronto Raptors to new heights. In the history of the franchise, no player has ever led the Raptors to the Conference Finals. Vince Carter could not do it. Chris Bosh could not do it. It would take DeMar DeRozan to take them to the deepest playoff run in franchise history. Of course, he had a lot of help on the way. Kyle Lowry was just as valuable, if not more valuable, than DeRozan was for the team. Their role players and coaching staff were also among the best the franchise had ever fielded. DeMar DeRozan was part of the history that was unfolding for the Toronto Raptors.

The problem for the Toronto Raptors as they were heading into the Conference Finals was that they were on their way to face one of the championship favorites that season. The Cleveland Cavaliers, led by LeBron James, had dominated the entire playoff landscape by sweeping the first two rounds. While they were not the best team in the regular season, the playoffs were a much different since everyone on the Cavs' roster was clicking on all cylinders. The scariest part was that they had the best player in the world.

Other than facing a powerhouse title favorite squad, the problem for the Toronto Raptors was that they were probably out of gas. In contrast to the Cavaliers, who had played only eight games the entire playoffs, the Raptors had to play 14 tough playoff games in the first two rounds. Their core duo of DeRozan and Lowry were also getting beat up on a lot of plays considering that the Raptors were relying the most on them. While they still had a lot of fight in them, the odds were not in Toronto's favor.

At first, it looked like the Cavaliers were on their way to another series sweep. The Raptors could not withstand the offensive assault of the Cavaliers. While DeMar DeRozan would have a respectable 18-point performance in Game 1, the rest of the team was unable to stop the Cavs from imposing their will on the Raptors. Toronto would end up losing that game by 31 points.

Game 2 was not much different. Though DeRozan was again playing well with his 22 points on a decent shooting clip, he was the lone bright spot on the starting squad. The bench players were even better than all the starters save for DeMar

DeRozan. In the end, the starters' lack of production contributed to another loss as the Cavaliers were looking like they were on their way to another sweep.

The problem with the Toronto Raptors in those first two games was the lack of production by Kyle Lowry and the other role players. During the entire playoffs, it was a rarity to see both DeRozan and Lowry playing excellent basketball on the same night. If they were both playing well, the other players tended to follow suit. If they wanted to extend the series, the two backcourt players had to explode together on the same night.

When the series shifted to Canada for Games 3 and 4, the Toronto Raptors suddenly looked inspired. DeMar DeRozan was hitting his shots from the field. Kyle Lowry was making his three-pointers. The bench was also contributing well to the cause. But the biggest story of the night was backup center Bismack Biyombo, who was filling in for the injured Jonas Valanciunas. Despite being undersized at 6'9", Biyombo was doing his best Ben Wallace impersonation by defending the paint well and attracting all the rebounds. He ended up with 26 rebounds and four blocks in that contest. Meanwhile, DeRozan top scored with 32 points on 12 out of 24 shooting.

In Game 4, the backcourt duo of the Raptors finally stepped up to the plate to explode on the same night. Throughout the season, DeMar DeRozan and Kyle Lowry were regarded as one of the best backcourt tandems in the league. They were also the second-highest backcourt duo in the entire NBA. Only the Golden State Warriors' Stephen Curry and Klay Thompson were arguably better than them. After the Raptors' duo, no other backcourt in the entire league came close to their production and star power, and this was evident in Game 4.

The offense revolved around both DeRozan and Lowry in that match. DeMarre Carroll was the only other player in double digits as the backcourt tandem took it upon themselves to score big on every possession. Despite the obvious fact that the plays were going to be called either for DeRozan or Lowry, the Cavaliers could not stop any of them. DeRozan would shoot 14 out of 23 from the field to score 32 points. Meanwhile, Kyle Lowry had his best game of the series by going for 35 points on a 14 out of 20 shooting clip from the field. With that kind of a backcourt explosion, the Toronto Raptors were able to tie the series up 2-2.

Despite the tough fight that the Raptors put up in those two home games in Toronto, the Cleveland Cavaliers went into championship mode and immediately pounded their opponents in the next two games. They won Game 5 by 38 points. While Game 6 was played in Toronto, the Cavs would end up winning the series by dominating the Raptors by 26. That loss in Game 6 ended what was the best season in franchise history and for any of the players in the Toronto Raptors' locker room. Cleveland eventually won the 2016 NBA title.

While the Toronto Raptors' season may have ended without an appearance in the NBA Finals, the team had a lot of positives they could take from that season. First, they won their franchise-best 56 games and were as high as the second seed in the Eastern Conference. Second, they were beginning to click as a team that had a combination of veteran talent and young role players. And third, they saw the growth of one of the best backcourt duos in the NBA.

Combining for nearly 44 points per game, DeMar DeRozan and Kyle Lowry were the second best scoring backcourt in the league that season. They were also considered the best overall backcourt duo in the NBA and were only behind the Golden State Warriors' shooting duo in that category. Both were All-Stars in the same season, and both were considered the best players on the roster. What set them apart was how well they complimented each other. Lowry was a good playmaker and outside shooter. He brought toughness to the backcourt with his defense and pit bull personality. Meanwhile, DeRozan was the solid scoring punch that delivered from the perimeter and in the paint. He was their go-to guy whenever they needed shots in tough situations. They played and fed well off of each other's strengths and weaknesses. Lowry brought in the outside shooting that DeRozan was hesitant with. Meanwhile, DeRozan had the athleticism that Lowry did not have. The scary part about the duo was that they were only going to get better.

## The Road to Becoming Elite

Working from the positives of what was a productive 2015-16 season, the Toronto Raptors were still regarded as one of the teams to beat in the East coming into the 2016-17 season. Though they would lose Luis Scola in the offseason, the new rookies and other veteran forwards were ready to step up. The core role players were secured while the starters were established as the key players coming into the new season. And while both DeRozan and Lowry had a great season as a tandem the previous year, nobody expected the jump they made.

Though Kyle Lowry had an increase in production that season, the best improvement was on the part of DeMar DeRozan. Already a much-improved player the past season, the two-time All-Star was not content with what he had as far as skillset was concerned. With Kobe Bryant enjoying retirement, DeRozan had a Mamba mantle to carry. He was going to put the same maniacal work into his game as his childhood hero did, especially after signing a ridiculously large $139 million five-year extension to stay in Toronto.

The improvement to DeRozan's game started in Rio de Janeiro where he was one of the players selected to take part in the 2016 Olympics as a member of Team USA's basketball team. Apart from participating in the team's training regiments and usual exercises and practice, DeMar DeRozan was one of the few players that went beyond the call of duty during that summer.

DeRozan would wake up at 5:30 in the morning to start his daily training. His first focus was to go to the weight room to add more meat to his already muscular frame. He wanted to stay lean, but also get bigger and stronger. He hit the weight room and pool hard to get to his ideal body goal. He remained at his normal 220-pound weight but had more muscle than he ever did by making a change in his diet.[vii] He cut out a lot of fat to stay lean and strong just like how teammate Kyle Lowry did a year before. He would also say that he had the toughest summer of his life while all other NBA players were enjoying the break.

While not necessarily making significant changes to his game, DeMar DeRozan absorbed a lot of confidence and knowledge from 11 of the best players in the world during his run with Team USA that summer. He learned from some of the best peers who were on his level or even better than him. Some would think that he was lazy during those practices with Team USA because he was merely observing his other teammates. But DeRozan took the Bryant approach by studying his Olympic teammates (and NBA rival). He was using the mental approach in trying to make himself a better player that season. DeMar took that knowledge and confidence to the NBA once the season started.[vii]

DeMar DeRozan immediately made his presence felt as soon as the season started. He would open the new campaign by going for 40 points on 17 out of 27 shooting from the field in a win over the Detroit Pistons. The man would not slow down after going for 32 in a loss to the Cleveland Cavaliers on October 28. He then had 33 in his third game followed by a 40-point performance against the Wizards on November 2. He made 14 of his 23 field goals in that match. His run of five consecutive games of scoring at least 30 points ended after winning a game against Miami. He had 34 in that bout. With that performance against the Heat, DeMar DeRozan set a franchise record for most consecutive games of scoring at least 30 points.

But DeMar DeRozan did not slow down a bit after going for only 23 points after that game against the Heat. He would have 37 points in a win over the Oklahoma City Thunder on November 9. He followed that up with 34 in a win over the Charlotte Hornets. DeRozan would then torch the New York Knicks for 33 points in his ninth game of the season. His hot start earned him his second Player of the Week award.

Nine games into the regular season and DeMar DeRozan was averaging about 34 points per night. He had eight games of scoring at least 30 points in those first nine games alone. While the Raptors' wingman was idolizing Kobe Bryant for most of his life, people saw flashes of Michael Jordan himself in DeMar DeRozan after that fantastic start to the season.

The last person in the history of the league to start the season with five consecutive games of scoring at least 30 points was Michael Jordan back in 1986, even before DeMar DeRozan was born.[viii] DeRozan was wreaking havoc out there on the floor while already making half of the 30-point games he had two seasons ago. It was a clear sign of his improvement over the offseason.

Raptors head coach Dwane Casey credits DeRozan's fantastic start to the season with the body development he had over the summer. With his new strength, he was not afraid to absorb contact when finishing baskets at the rim. He was taking more shots inside the paint rather than pulling up for contested midrange jumpers out on the perimeter. DeRozan became more methodical and picky with his shot selection. He was not going to let a little contact get in the way of finishing baskets at the rim.[vi] Adding the fact that he was in the prime of his athletic form and DeMar DeRozan had become an unstoppable offensive force.

While DeMar DeRozan may have had a fantastic start to the season, his numbers would see a dip as fatigue took its toll and the adrenaline rush was slowing down. Teams began to focus and adjust their defenses accordingly to DeRozan. His production would take a dip late in November, but he was still one of the top scorers in the league.

Come December, DeMar DeRozan resumed his scoring tear and went for 30 points in five games he played that month. That included four consecutive games of scoring 30 points in the middle of December. He started with 30 against the Milwaukee Bucks before going for 31 in Philadelphia on December 14. He then had 34 points two days later against the Atlanta Hawks while ending the run with 31 in only 30 minutes against the Orlando Magic. The Raptors would only lose one game during that run.

It was also during December when DeMar DeRozan made Raptors franchise history. In a loss to the Golden State Warriors on December 28, DeRozan would score a total of 29 points to surpass Chris Bosh as the all-time scoring leader of the team. He had not only become the best scorer in Toronto Raptors history but its best player as well. He had the All-Star appearances and team accomplishments to bolster his claim to that mantle.

Early in January of 2017, DeMar DeRozan would have a string of three great performances. He would go for 36 points on 10 out of 23 shooting from the field in a loss to the Chicago Bulls on January 7. The following night, he went for 36 points, six rebounds, and five assists in a loss to the Houston Rockets. That was his 18th 30-point game of the season. He would cap that run with 41 points and a career-best 13 rebounds in a win over the Boston Celtics on January 10.

On January 17, DeMar DeRozan would be voted in by fans as a starter for the 2017 All-Star Game, becoming the fourth Raptor to so. Late in January, however, he would miss a few games because of a minor injury. He would miss seven games but would still come back healthy after resting it out during those missed outings. In DeRozan's return on February 6, he would go for 31 points on 11 out of 22 shooting from the field in a win against the Los Angeles Clippers. He followed that up with 30 points in a loss to the Minnesota Timberwolves just a day later.

In his first game following the All-Star break, DeMar DeRozan would post a new career high in points. He forced his way to lead a 17-point deficit comeback against the Boston Celtics in that game on February 24. He made 15 of his 28 field goal attempts and all 12 of his free throws to score a total of 43 points. He also added five rebounds and five assists to his name. In the game after that, he would go for 33 versus the Portland Trailblazers. Then, on February 27, he went for 37 points against the New York Knicks. Both were wins.

On March 3, DeMar DeRozan would go for a rare double-double. Using all of his athleticism, DeRozan finished the game with 13 rebounds. He also had 32 points while shooting 10 out of 17 from the floor and hitting all three of the three-point shots he attempted. The Raptors would end up winning that game against the Washington Wizards.

For a fifth time that season, DeMar DeRozan would go for another 40-point game. In a win against the Chicago Bulls on March 21, he would hit 17 of his 38 shots to finish with 42 points and 8 rebounds. Two days later, he would go for back-to-back 40-point games. DeRozan would lead the Raptors in a win over the Miami Heat by going 14 out of 25 from the field to finish the game with 40 big points.

Proving for the final time during the regular season that he had grown into an elite scorer that could put up 40 points on any given night, DeMar DeRozan would go for 40 points on 11 out of 26 shooting from the field in a win over the Indiana Pacers on March 31. He also made 15 of the 20 free throws he attempted that night.

DeMar DeRozan would finish the regular season with career highs of 27.3 points and 5.2 rebounds in addition to the 3.9 assists and 1.1 steals he was averaging. He improved by nearly four points a game precisely because he was shooting and making more of his shots. He had improved his field goal shooting to 46.7%, which is the highest he has ever had since becoming an All-Star.

In addition to his improved numbers, DeRozan's backcourt mate Kyle Lowry also improved his production. And with the shared scoring going on in Toronto, DeRozan and Lowry surpassed the duo of Curry and Thompson as the best scoring backcourt in the NBA. They combined for a total of nearly 50 points per game. At that point of their respective careers, they may even been the best backcourt tandem in the league.

Under DeRozan's and Lowry's leadership, the Toronto Raptors finished the regular season with a record of 51 wins against 31 losses. They were once again a top contender in the Eastern Conference after securing the third seed. And because DeRozan had proven himself to be among the elite players in the league that season, it was time for him and the Raptors to prove that they could take their game to the next level in the playoffs.

Often criticized as a great regular season team but a subpar playoff squad, the Toronto Raptors would face stiff competition in the first round of the postseason. The Milwaukee Bucks would beat the Raptors in Game 1 and DeMar DeRozan finished with 27 points and eight rebounds while shooting only 7 out of 21 from the floor. Nevertheless, DeRozan had a respectable outing in Game 2 to give the Raptors a win.

DeRozan would have arguably the worse playoff game in his entire career in Game 3 in Milwaukee. In that blowout loss to the Bucks, who would go on to secure a 2-1 lead, DeMar shot 0 out of 8 from the floor and scored all of his eight points from the free throw line. While it was not DeRozan's fault that the Raptors lost, as the leader of the team, he knew he should have done much better than that.

Not willing to fall into a deeper hole, DeMar DeRozan would put it on himself to win Game 4 in Milwaukee. In that 11-point win for the Raptors, DeRozan went for 12 out of 22 from the field to finish the game with 33 points, nine rebounds, five assists, and four huge steals. He would then help give the series lead to the Raptors with a win in Game 5.

With a chance to finish the series in six games, DeMar DeRozan had to play one of his best games. He needed every point in that three-point win for the Raptors as the All-Star wingman made 12 of his 22 field goals to score 32 points. Though he performed well on the offensive end, it was his defense that helped his team secure the win. DeRozan had his hands all over the passing lanes and was hounding his defensive assignment to submission. He ended the series-clinching win with a total of five steals as the Toronto Raptors qualified for the second round of the playoffs.

Unfortunately for DeMar DeRozan, he and his squad would have to face the defending champions and the man that had given them problems in the playoffs every time they saw each other—the Cleveland Cavaliers and LeBron James. Despite how much the Raptors have improved each season, they never seemed to perform well against the Cleveland Cavaliers. But this season, they thought they had the chance to make things harder for LeBron, especially with the addition of defensive specialist PJ Tucker.

But Game 1 seemed like an indication of what the series was going to be for the Raptors. They could not solve the offensive attack of the Cavaliers and could not score the ball effectively themselves. DeRozan was limited to only 7 out of 16 from the floor in what was a 19-point scoring game for him. Game 2, which was another loss, was even more difficult for DeMar DeRozan. He finished with only five points in what was another horrible performance for him. Toronto would lose that game by 22 points.

In did not even matter that the Raptors moved the series back to Toronto for Games 3 and 4 because the Cavs just had their number. Despite the bounce back 37-point game from DeRozan, Toronto still lost by a large margin as the Cavs secured an insurmountable 3-0 lead. The Raptors looked like they tried to fight hard in Game 4 but it was all for nothing. DeMar DeRozan, for a second straight year, would bow out of the playoffs at the hands of LeBron James and the Cleveland Cavaliers.

Though the Toronto Raptors could not get that deep playoff run they were hoping for, what cannot be argued at that moment was that their best player had evolved into an elite star in the league. DeMar DeRozan had proven that year that he could score with the best of them and that he could lead a team to a good record in the regular season. He was the league's best scoring shooting guard (if James Harden was counted as a point guard that season) and became a premier midrange player much like his idol Kobe Bryant.

DeRozan was looking more like Bryant more and more as his offensive repertoire was evolving. He could take any defender off the dribble to drain midrange shots over an outstretched arm or attack the basket strong with the drive. At the post, he had shown improvements to his ability to turn around and hit a fading basket. And with the way he was taking over a lot of games, he was showing a bit of the killer instinct that made Bryant so deadly in his prime.

However, even Kobe Bryant needed help to win championships. And while DeMar DeRozan had an All-Star caliber playmaker in Kyle Lowry, the role players and the bench needed to step up.

Outside of DeRozan and Lowry, the Raptors could not find consistent production. Midseason acquisition Serge Ibaka and center Jonas Valanciunas were capable in their own ways, but they were not explosive scorers that could carry the load whenever the star backcourt was not doing well.

## The Final Year in Toronto

If there was a clear weakness to the Raptors' game last season, it was that they were nothing if DeRozan and Lowry were performing subpar. They did not have a lot of weapons outside of their starting five. But that was the biggest change they were going to implement during the 2017-18 season. Though DeRozan was still in the prime of his career and as elite as any other shooting guard can be, he did not have to do it alone.

Dwane Casey and the rest of the coaching staff empowered the Toronto Raptors bench and learn to rely more on the role players instead of just the stars and core starters. DeMar DeRozan himself would also transform himself into a player that relies more on the people around him rather on himself alone. He would not have the same kind of hot start that he had a year ago but DeRozan was just as effective as he ever was in leading a team that could score all around.

DeRozan's early season-high was when he had 30 points in a 34-point win against the Philadelphia 76ers on October 21, 2017. In that game, he made 8 of his 12 shots and 14 of his 16 free throws in only less than 27 minutes that night. He would outperform himself on November 3 in a game against the Utah Jazz. On that night, he had 37 points on a 50% field goal shooting from the field. He also made all 14 of his free throws.

Despite the fact that he was still scoring as well as an elite star should, DeRozan was also passing the ball as if he was a point guard. On November 9, he had 33 points and a season-high of eight assists in a win over the New Orleans Pelicans. Then, over the next five games, he had five or more assists four times. The only time he did not have at least five assists was a loss for the Toronto Raptors. His passing, as well as his scoring, have both become barometers for the Raptors' wins.

Nevertheless, scoring was still the name of the game and DeMar DeRozan was still among the best in the league at that department. On December 13, he would go for 12 out of 24 from the field to tie his season-high of 37 points in a win over the Phoenix Suns. However, he would have an even better scoring performance just a few days after that.

Showing that he had taken his game to the next level by extending his range all the way to the three-point area, DeMar DeRozan would hit 6 out of 9 three-pointers in a win over the Philadelphia 76ers on December 21. He finished that game making 13 of his 21 shots and 13 of his 15 free throws to score a new season high of 45 points. But that still was not the icing on the cake.

In just his first game of the year 2018, DeMar DeRozan exploded once more for a great scoring performance. In that win over the Milwaukee Bucks on January 1, DeRozan hit 17 of his 29 field goals, 5 of his 9 three-pointers, and all 13 of his free throws to finish the game with new career-high of 52 points. He also ended up with eight assists in what is arguably DeMar DeRozan's greatest performance as a professional basketball player.

If there was a reason as to why and how DeMar DeRozan continued to improve that season, it was that he was taking and making more three-pointers. As basketball continues to evolve, success has been closely tied to the three-point shot. The 2012 and 2013 championship teams of the Miami Heat had three-point shooters waiting in the wings for whenever LeBron James and Dwyane Wade broke defenses down. The 2014 championship teams of the San Antonio Spurs relied on ball movement to open up shooters. Steve Kerr's Golden State Warriors then took that strategy to the next level and won the 2015 and 2017 championships by making the three-point shot their primary weapon.

In 2018, a lot more teams have learned to use the three-point shot more and more. The Houston Rockets, with James Harden and Chris Paul, lived and died by the three-pointer and led the entire NBA in three-point shots made and taken during the 2017-18 season as they were also able to secure the best record in the league with that kind of a strategy. The Cleveland Cavaliers, on their part, also continue to surround LeBron James with shooters that could break games wide open in an instant.

All the best players in the league also rely heavily on the three-point shot. LeBron James takes and makes three-point shots to make sure defenders do not sag off him. Kevin Durant, arguably the best scorer in the league, uses the three-point shot in a deadly manner especially because he stands almost seven feet tall and has a 7'5" wingspan. James Harden led the league in scoring during the 2017-18 season by making the step-back three-point shot a big part of his game. And we all know that Stephen Curry and Klay Thompson are both the league's best three-point shooters. Even big men such as DeMarcus Cousins,

Karl-Anthony Towns, and Joel Embiid occasionally step out to shoot long-range baskets.

But for DeMar DeRozan, the three-point shot has never been a significant part of his game. Driving to the basket, drawing fouls, and hitting midrange jumpers were always how he effectively put points on the board. But he has never learned how to use the three-point shot to his advantage. Before the 2017-18 season, he had only taken 1.4 three-pointers per game and made 28% of them in eight seasons in the league because the midrange shot was his bread and butter. In comparison, his idol Kobe Bryant took at least four three-pointers a game in an era when the shot was not as big of a part of the game as it is today.

Other than because he could still put points up on the board without the help of the three-point shot, DeMar DeRozan was not taking three-pointers because his coach did not force him to do so. The only reason why DeRozan was even making three-pointers in the past seasons was that he was just shooting the ball without looking at where he was on the floor. But as the NBA continues to evolve, what was clear was that DeMar DeRozan needed to expand his game.

Though he knew that the league heavily relies on the three-point shot, Dwane Casey did not like forcing his star to shoot three-pointers because he knew DeRozan could still perform at his best as a midrange shooter. For DeMar's part, he was already confident in his game and how great he was as a strict midrange shooter. But he and Casey both knew that he should be better at an aspect of the game he was never comfortable with. He needed to develop a three-point shot.

DeMar DeRozan, during the offseason, took a good look at his game and realized that he was shooting a lot of long midrange shots, which are considered the most inefficient shots in the game. Why would anyone take shots a foot away from the three-point line instead of just extending all the way outside the perimeter? DeRozan asked himself that very same question and realized that he could be more efficient and effective if he just decided to take three-pointers instead of long midrange shots.[ix]

Saying that he wanted to simplify the game and make it easier for him, DeMar DeRozan cut down his long two-pointers by half and has made more three-pointers for the Toronto Raptors.

He constantly worked on his three-point shot by locking himself in the gym at night and shoot jumpers until he could no longer stand. But the best part of his development was how Casey trusted him. The Toronto Raptors head coach never forced DeRozan to quickly develop himself into a three-point threat. Instead, he was patient and trusted DeMar's style of play as long as the All-Star was producing. And now in his ninth season in the league, DeMar DeRozan has taken that trust and has transformed himself into an all-around shooting threat.

Fresh off another All-Star appearance, DeMar DeRozan made the Toronto Raptors a more dangerous team in the second of the season not only because he had become a better shooter but because he had become a better all-around star. The Raptors would only lose six games after the All-Star break and it was thanks in large part to how DeRozan has learned to defer and trust his teammates.

The 2017-18 Toronto Raptors were revamped version of themselves as far as style and strategy were concerned. They kept the same core group of players but were able to bolster the team with an empowered bench. The Raptors had a solid starting core of DeRozan, Lowry, Anunoby, Ibaka, and Valanciunas but the bench players stepped up whenever they were needed. The Raptors were constantly one of the highest scoring teams in the league thanks to the balanced bench production they were getting from the likes of Fred VanVleet, Pascal Siakam, CJ Miles, and Delon Wright. They had the third-highest scoring bench in the league and had the best bench scorers among all of the playoff contenders.

The improved bench production was what helped DeMar DeRozan evolve into a better player and leader. Because he had players he could trust, DeRozan was not only shooting better but was also passing the ball at a career rate. Even when he was scoring big, he was still finding his teammates for open shots. For example, when he scored 42 points in a win over the Detroit Pistons on March 7, DeRozan finished with six assists. There were even instances where he did not have to score much because the bench was there to help him.

At the end of the season, DeMar DeRozan averaged 23 points, which was lower than the production he had last season. However, there was no arguing that he had become a more effective and efficient player. DeRozan shot 3.6 three-point attempts that season and had made just as many three-pointers as he has had in the previous two seasons combined. On top of all that, his shot selection improved and he was taking fewer long midrange shots and opted to take more three-pointers instead. He was doing that while averaging only 34 minutes, the lowest since his rookie year.

As a mark of a true leader, DeMar DeRozan also averaged a career-best 5.2 assists that season. He never even averaged more than four assists a game before that season. This was because DeRozan had become an integral part of a system that revolves around his ability to create for himself and others. Everyone knows how good of a shot maker DeRozan is. But he has evolved into playmaker that empowered the Raptors' dangerous bench.

Arguably the most impressive improvement to DeMar DeRozan's game was how he changed his mindset. For a very long time, he was the subject of criticisms. He was called one-dimensional, overpaid, and a waste of athleticism. After all, he relied more on his midrange shot and did not dominate athletically like LeBron James and Russell Westbrook do. But the biggest criticism to his game was that he is a relic of the past and an old-fashioned player that belongs in a different era.

However, DeMar DeRozan has learned to shrug off all of those criticisms and keep his eye on the prize. The All-Star guard does not let critics affect the way he plays, though he always knew that sacrifices will always be a big part of winning a championship.[x] Criticisms were not what led DeRozan to change his game, but it was the thought of winning a title that made him want to shoot more three-pointers and play more as a passer and delegator.

There are not a lot of clear differences between how DeRozan and Bryant play. What was always evident was how Bryant was always more of a competitor and a leader. But, during the 2017-18 season, DeMar DeRozan was able to lessen the gap between him and Bryant as far as leadership and competitive edge was concerned. That was how the Toronto Raptors won a franchise record of 59 wins and the best record in the Eastern Conference.

Once again, the true test of the Toronto Raptors' grit was the postseason, where they have never performed as well as they did compared to the regular season. But Games 1 and 2 were indications of how far the Raptors have come. They defeated the eighth-seeded Washington Wizards by 19 points in total in those two games. While he did not have a great performance in Game 1, DeRozan finished Game 2 with 37 big points.

Nevertheless, the Washington Wizards bounced back hard in their home floor to win Games 3 and 4 and to tie the series two wins apiece. Once again, the Toronto Raptors could not escape criticism. They were the best team in the East during the regular season but were unable to perform well enough to escape a scare from the eighth-seeded team in a weaker Eastern Conference.

Not willing to cede the series lead to the Wizards, DeMar DeRozan stepped up big to finish Game 5 with 32 points and five assists. And while he did not have the best of games in Game 6, his 16 points were enough to give the Toronto Raptors a ten-point win. That win pushed them to the second round, where they would have to once again face their playoff tormentors.

The Cleveland Cavaliers were only the fourth-seeded team that season and were without Kyrie Irving. What was even more difficult was that LeBron James was virtually carrying a revamped squad on his own. Meanwhile, the Raptors had two All-Stars performing at peak level. They also had better supporting players and a higher-scoring bench. But what they did not have was an answer for LeBron James.

For a third consecutive year, the Toronto Raptors could not exorcise themselves of their demon, a man called The King. LeBron James seemingly destroyed the Raptors by his lonesome. Basketball is not a one-man sport and the best way for the Raptors to deal with LeBron was for their best player to perform at peak level. Unfortunately, DeRozan could not play up to par.

He had respectable outings in Games 1 and 2 but was a disappearing act in Games 3 and 4.

After averaging 23 points during the regular season and 26.7 points in the series against the Washington Wizards, DeMar DeRozan averaged only 17 points against the Cavaliers. What was worse was that he combined for only 21 points on an 8 out of 23 shooting clip from the field in Games 3 and 4. Because of how poorly he was performing in that series, there was no wonder that the Toronto Raptors were once again swept out of the playoffs by the Cleveland Cavaliers.

The greatest season in franchise history had gone to waste as both Dwane Casey and the Raptors core players became the subject of criticism. It was time for the team to go in a different direction either with Casey or some of the key players out of the team. Unfortunately for the coach, he was the first one to go as the Raptors decided to fire him even after becoming the frontrunner and eventual winner of the Coach of the Year award. But Dwane Casey was not the only big name in Toronto that the franchise let go.

## The Trade to San Antonio

During the offseason of 2018, the biggest news was about LeBron James' free agency and his eventual decision to sign with the Los Angeles Lakers. After all, he was still the best player in the league and could make the biggest impact among all of the players in the NBA. The second biggest news was arguably Kawhi Leonard's request for the San Antonio Spurs to trade him.

The two-time Defensive Player of the Year and one of the best players in the world had grown unhappy in San Antonio after he and the organization could not see eye-to-eye regarding Leonard's health and future with the team. Kawhi Leonard would specifically request to be traded to the Los Angeles Lakers. However, the Spurs did not want to trade one of the best players in the world to a Western Conference rival. Instead, they looked to the East for a suitable trading partner.

Several Eastern Conference teams rose up as suitors for the services of Kawhi Leonard. The Boston Celtics, who were already good enough to force the Cavs to a seven-game series in the Eastern Conference Finals despite missing their two best players, were frontrunners at one point. When trade talks with the Celtics died down, the Philadelphia 76ers thought they could make a trade for the two-way specialist. However, they would not end up with the services of Kawhi Leonard. Instead, an unlikely team became the destination of the superstar forward.

In what was one of the most surprising trades, the San Antonio Spurs would send Kawhi Leonard to the Toronto Raptors in exchange for center Jakob Poeltl, a first-round pick, and none other than the face of the franchise. The two teams shocked the world as DeMar DeRozan was sent to the San Antonio Spurs as part of what was thought to be the Raptors' decision to move the franchise in a different direction.

While it was not shocking that Leonard was traded, the shocking part was that DeRozan had been moved. The All-Star guard himself was in disbelief. DeMar DeRozan was happy in Toronto and wanted to stay a Raptor all his life. Every move he made in the offseason was so that he could improve for the sake of the Toronto Raptors. Never in his wildest dreams did he believe that he would be traded. The organization even assured him that he was not going to be traded. Toronto was his home and it was where his heart and loyalty lied. Some players even took to social media to express their shock.[xi]

But at the end of the day, the NBA is a business. Every decision the franchise makes is supposed to be towards making the team even better in the hopes of winning a championship. As seen from how the Raptors were unable to go deeper into the playoffs or even beat LeBron and the Cavs, it was clear that the direction they were heading toward was not the right one. For the business to succeed, they needed to make some changes. The first change was to let Casey go, and the second one was to deal their franchise icon for another star.

Critics would say that DeRozan planted his own grave in Toronto. He was getting paid a huge sum to perform well and to put the team in position for a title. However, all that he and his teammates ever produced were two consecutive four-game losses to the Cleveland Cavaliers in the last two seasons. The final nail on the coffin for DeMar DeRozan was probably his humiliatingly poor performance against the Cavs in the 2018 playoffs. No matter how loyal he has been to the Toronto Raptors, family is but a word in the business of sports.[xii] The foremost goal is to produce titles, which DeRozan was unable to give to Toronto.

Nevertheless, it was a rare sight for the Toronto Raptors to actually trade a star that wanted to play with them. Back in the day, Vince Carter forced himself to a trade that sent him from Toronto to New Jersey. Then, Chris Bosh left in 2010 to form a trio of stars in Miami. But despite having a lot of options and with no obligation to stay in Toronto as long as he did, DeMar DeRozan decided to give his loyalty to the Raptors for nine whole seasons.

Because of what DeRozan has done in Toronto and with the way he has led the Raptors to their most successful regular season records, many would consider that he has already become the best player in franchise history. While some would say that he was never the greatest player the franchise has seen, there is still no argument that he is the most loyal star to ever play for the Canada-based team.

But loyalty can only get you so far. DeMar DeRozan is no longer a Raptor but is now a member of the San Antonio Spurs, arguably the best team and the most consistent franchise in the NBA for the last 20 years. Being in San Antonio not only puts him in position to play for one of the most well-run organizations in the league but also to learn under Gregg Popovich, one of the best coaches in the history of the NBA.

Popovich said that he was excited to coach DeMar DeRozan.[xiii] After missing Leonard's services last season and relying more on LaMarcus Aldridge's stellar performance, the five-time champion coach led the team to a seventh seed in the playoffs. But what can he do with two All-Stars, particularly with an All-NBA shooting guard teaming up with an All-NBA big man?

On offense, DeRozan closely resembles what Leonard could do. He is a great pick-and-roll player, a guy that can do well in isolation situations, and someone that can produce anywhere on the floor. DeRozan is an unselfish and unassuming player that fits well within the San Antonio Spurs' culture. As he is a terrific all-around talent that does not come with a big ego or a selfish personality, he is a guy that fits the mold of what the Spurs look for in their stars.

Paired with LaMarcus Aldridge, DeMar DeRozan will give an inside-outside presence to the Spurs. The criticism is that he and Aldridge are both old school players at their respective positions. However, the Spurs have always won titles in the most uncanny of ways. No matter how traditional DeRozan's playing style may be, he is still an All-NBA talent and one of the best shooting guards in the league. Still 28 and as hardworking as ever, his game might see greater heights under one of the best coaches in the history of the league.

# Chapter 5: International Career

DeMar DeRozan has been one of the fixtures for the Team USA basketball team program. He first joined the program back in 2012 as part of a pool of selected young players. Since then, he has regularly been training with the USA Basketball program and would make the roster cut in 2014. He made his international basketball debut during the 2014 FIBA World Cup held in Spain. During that tournament, he joined James Harden and Klay Thompson, who were the two other shooting guards known to be the best the NBA could offer.

Since Team USA focused on a running style of play during the 2014 FIBA World Cup, they were not short of guards and wing players. This led to short stints for DeMar DeRozan as the team had a bevy of point guards and wingmen to choose from. He averaged only 4.8 points in the nine games he played in that tournament. His best output was when he had 11 points in 18 minutes of action against the Dominican Republic. Team USA was undefeated the entire tournament on their way to a gold medal finish.

DeMar DeRozan would return to international action in 2016 as a member of the team that went to Rio de Janeiro in Brazil to participate in the 2016 Olympics. He was another key wing player in Team USA's quest to outrun the competition every single play. His best performance that tournament was when he had 11 points in only ten minutes of action in Team USA's elimination round win against a gritty Serbia team that nearly beat them. DeRozan averaged 6.6 points the entire tournament and won his first Olympic gold medal.

# Chapter 6: Personal Life

DeMar DeRozan was born in Compton, California to his parents Frank and Diane. Frank used to be a professional football player, though he would not reach stardom in that department. Both of DeMar's parents' have athletic backgrounds, which gave him an edge as far as size and athleticism were concerned. DeMar's parents have always been supportive of their son's basketball dreams ever since he was a young boy. DeMar would later raise a family of his own. He has two daughters with his fiancée Kiara Morrison. The first, Diar, was born in 2013. The second one, Mari, was born in 2015.

DeMar DeRozan's favorite athlete since he was old enough to play basketball has always been Kobe Bryant. He watched Laker games as a boy living near Los Angeles. He closely followed and monitored Bryant's every moment and move while imitating and emulating the Laker star's skillset. DeRozan also wears Kobe Bryant's signature line of sneakers while wearing the number 10 jersey in honor of his idol's jersey number as a member of Team USA. Kobe Bryant impacted DeRozan's game the most as his playing style and moves are reflected in how DeMar plays the sport. As a token of his appreciation to the man that influenced his game the most, DeRozan gave Bryant a commemorative Spalding basketball back in December of 2016.

Outside of the NBA, DeMar DeRozan has several personal endeavors and charity works. He formed the DeMar DeRozan Slam Dunk Book Club back when he was still a rookie. The purpose of the book club was to teach the importance of reading to a select school in Toronto. Aside from reading, the club also showed that reading, studying, and basketball can all be done simultaneously. He has regularly contributed free tickets and basketball merchandise to the program and the school while also trying to improve its sports and literacy programs.

DeMar DeRozan, during the offseasons, often spends his day back in Los Angeles near his hometown of Compton to participate in grassroots basketball tournaments such as the Drew League, where he has been competing since he was 14 years old. He is also often seen playing pickup basketball in ballparks across L.A. and even Toronto.

# Chapter 7: Impact on Basketball

When it comes to DeMar DeRozan's impact as a basketball player, one should look at how far he got in the NBA from his humble beginnings in Compton, CA. Since he was in high school, DeMar DeRozan was always fond of choosing his path as a basketball player. He selected a lesser-known Compton High School over bigger names so that he could carve his legacy. And in college, he chose USC over other potentially better programs so that he could become his own man.

When he came to the NBA, nobody thought he could blossom into an elite star in the league. Everybody knew he was good and had the potential to become a star if honed correctly. But he was largely a raw athletic specimen in his rookie year. He did not have the right tools or skills to excel right away. He was a project player that the Toronto Raptors were patient with. He bided his time and tried to develop his game his way.

When the time was right, DeMar DeRozan blossomed into an All-Star that led his team back to the playoffs after a five-year drought. He was making Raptor history every single year he played with the team. And it did not take long for him to become an elite player in the league after becoming an All-Star starter and one of the best scorers in the NBA in 2016.

The impact that DeMar DeRozan has on basketball is predicated on how hard he worked just to get to where he is right now. He was never the most sought-after player in his draft class. However, he worked hard on his game every year. He emulated Kobe Bryant's maniacal approach to improving his game from the mental and the physical aspects. He got to where he is not only because of the physical investments he made, but also with the mental approach he took to improve his knowledge, IQ, and confidence.

When one looks at DeMar DeRozan, one expected him to excel. After all, he is a 6'7" wingman that weighs 220 pounds of lean muscle. On top of that, he has all the athleticism in the world. But make no mistake about it, physical tools can only get you so far. DeRozan knew that. He focused on improving his skills since the very first day he stepped on an NBA hard floor. The product of such efforts was an elite All-Star, who could be regarded as the best player in Toronto Raptors history. And if the stars align for him in San Antonio, he could one day be considered one of the best wingmen in league history.

# Chapter 8: Legacy and Future

DeMar DeRozan continues on a legacy left by the most elite shooting guards in league history. Such a legacy started with the NBA logo himself, Jerry West. He passed it on to George Gervin, who went on to win three scoring titles with his unique skill set as a shooting guard. Gervin would pass the torch on to Michael Jordan, who made highlight reel plays every single season on his way to becoming widely considered the best player in the history of the game. Jordan would pass the mantle on to Kobe Bryant, who patterned his game after the Greatest of All-Time on his way to five NBA titles and numerous high-scoring moments.

In today's NBA, the modern version of the traditional elite shooting guard that was modeled after the likes of Gervin, Jordan, and Bryant comes in the form of DeMar DeRozan. DeRozan is as traditional as it gets. He attacks the basket frequently, much like how a young Michael Jordan did. He uses an arsenal of elegant finishes like Gervin did. He mastered the art of the midrange game much like how Bryant did. He has become an elite player all by himself even by refusing to adjust to the modern NBA style.

Today's NBA is predicated on the two most efficient places to score: inside the paint and outside the three-point area. While DeMar DeRozan thrives under and over the basket whenever he gets to the painted area, he has refused to become part of an NBA movement among guards and even big men that love to shoot the three-point bomb.

DeRozan is simply as traditional as it gets when it comes to shooting guards. It is not as if he is not an efficient shooter from the three-point area. It is just that he prefers pulling up from inside the perimeter much like how his basketball idols and predecessors did. Never has DeMar DeRozan taken a lot of three-pointers. Prior to the 2017-18 season, he only took 1.4 attempts from three-point range. He may have increased that number to 3.6 during the 2017-18 season but he still operated more in the perimeter. In comparison, fellow shooting guard James Harden shot ten attempts a game and 722 three-pointers during the 2017-18 season and made more than DeRozan ever has in his career. But DeMar DeRozan's refusal to shoot more three-pointers has never hindered him or his team from becoming elite contenders. The Toronto Raptors have always relied on him for the bulk of their points even though he does not shoot a lot of three-pointers. DeRozan is simply today's version of the traditional elite shooting guard.

Like Jordan and Kobe, DeRozan makes up for his lack of three-point shooting by going hard to the basket almost every play. He is one of the most fouled players in the league, much like how Bryant is the all-time leader in free throws among guards. DeRozan likes getting hit while absorbing contact in the paint. And on top of that, he has also learned how to play the post similar to how MJ and the Mamba did when they were getting wiser and older. His offensive arsenal shows how much DeMar DeRozan has learned from history to become the mirror image of the past generations' best wingmen.

With all the seasons he has played with the Toronto Raptors and all the years he spent developing with the team from the ground up, DeMar DeRozan is arguably the best player in franchise history. If you look at the all-time stats of the Toronto Raptors, DeRozan leads the pack concerning games played, minutes logged, and points scored. Nobody in franchise history has played more games and scored more points than DeMar DeRozan.

Vince Carter was the flashier and more popular player, and Chris Bosh was a better statistical player. But DeMar DeRozan's claim to the mantle of the best player in franchise history stems not from not only from the points he has scored for the team. It comes from the victories and deep playoff run he has led the team into. No other franchise player in Raptors history has ever led the team to record four new franchise records concerning wins. DeRozan did that three consecutive years until such time that he led the Raptors to its first 50-win season back in 2016. In the same year, he also led the team to the deepest playoff run it has ever gotten. And in 2018, he led the team to a 59-win season. Carter and Bosh might have both been better individual players, but they never got the Raptors as far as DeRozan has.

Now a member of the San Antonio Spurs, DeMar DeRozan carries with him the legacy of great players and of champions that were able to contribute so much to the franchise. He may become this generation's version of a George Gervin in San Antonio while giving championship hopes to the city the same way Robinson, Duncan, and Leonard did.

DeRozan is a perfect player to carry the San Antonio banner. He has the all-around perimeter skills of a Kawhi Leonard and the silent and unassuming qualities of a Tim Duncan. He is as humble and as unselfish as any San Antonio all-time great and may perhaps find himself in the same sentence as the champions and superstars that have donned the legendary Spurs uniform.

As far as DeMar DeRozan's future as a player is concerned, nobody could entirely gauge how far he can get. After all, nobody thought he would become a perennial All-Star someday. And nobody thought he would someday average nearly 28 points per game as one of the most elite players in the league. The sure thing is that he will continue to work hard on his game.

As of this writing, DeMar DeRozan is at the top of his athletic form. He uses his athleticism and his body very well to his advantage. However, what sets him apart is his dedication to the fundamental skills. He has improved his handles every single year. He has mastered the midrange game. He has learned how to play the post and with his back to the basket. He has developed an extensive array of finishing moves and artful finishes.

With those in mind, even as DeMar DeRozan's body would eventually diminish with age and the wear and tear of several tough NBA seasons, one would still expect him to be an active player. After all, both Jordan and Bryant were still elite players deep into their 30's because of their attention to the fundamental side of the game. They both honed their midrange game to perfection while also learning how to use their size and footwork down at the low post. DeRozan is following the same path and is on track to become just as effective as those all-time greats when he eventually ages.

And as DeMar DeRozan has been slowly but steadily embracing the three-point shot, we may one day see him become a more effective player though age may diminish his athletic gifts. Under Gregg Popovich's tutelage in San Antonio, he may even realize parts of his game he never thought he even had. It will not be a rare sight for him to see more All-NBA selections under San Antonio. But if he performs better than he did in Toronto and delivers a title under Pop's leadership, he may even be considered one of the all-time greats at his position when it is all said and done.

As DeMar DeRozan continues to carve his legacy as an NBA player, he has a chance to belong to a shortlist of the league's best shooting guards. It may be a short list, but one has to live up to names such as West, Gervin, Jordan, Drexler, Miller, Bryant, and Wade to belong to the elite shooting guard club. And since DeRozan still has a long way to go until he hangs his sneakers up, expect more All-Star appearances and playoff runs to come. Who knows? Maybe an NBA title that has eluded a lot of all-time greats might come his way in the future.

# Final Word/About the Author

I was born and raised in Norwalk, Connecticut. Growing up, I could often be found spending many nights watching basketball, soccer, and football matches with my father in the family living room. I love sports and everything that sports can embody. I believe that sports are one of most genuine forms of competition, heart, and determination. I write my works to learn more about influential athletes in the hopes that from my writing, you the reader can walk away inspired to put in an equal if not greater amount of hard work and perseverance to pursue your goals. If you enjoyed *DeMar DeRozan: The Inspiring Story of One of Basketball's Star Shooting Guards,* please leave a review! Also, you can read more of my works on *Roger Federer, Novak Djokovic, Andrew Luck, Rob Gronkowski, Brett Favre, Calvin Johnson, Drew Brees, J.J. Watt, Colin Kaepernick, Aaron Rodgers, Peyton Manning, Tom Brady, Russell Wilson, Michael Jordan, LeBron James, Kyrie Irving, Klay Thompson, Stephen Curry, Kevin Durant, Russell Westbrook, Anthony Davis, Chris Paul, Blake Griffin, Kobe Bryant, Joakim Noah, Scottie Pippen, Carmelo Anthony, Kevin Love, Grant Hill, Tracy McGrady, Vince Carter, Patrick Ewing, Karl Malone, Tony Parker, Allen Iverson, Hakeem Olajuwon, Reggie Miller, Michael Carter-Williams, John Wall, James Harden, Tim Duncan, Steve Nash,*

*Draymond Green, Kawhi Leonard, Dwyane Wade, Ray Allen, Pau Gasol, Dirk Nowitzki, Jimmy Butler, Paul Pierce, Manu Ginobili, Pete Maravich, Larry Bird, Kyle Lowry, Jason Kidd, David Robinson, LaMarcus Aldridge, Derrick Rose, Paul George, Kevin Garnett, Chris Paul, Marc Gasol, Yao Ming, Al Horford, Amar'e Stoudemire, Isaiah Thomas, Kemba Walker and Chris Bosh* in the Kindle Store. If you love basketball, check out my website at claytongeoffreys.com to join my exclusive list where I let you know about my latest books and give you lots of goodies.

# Like what you read? Please leave a review!

I write because I love sharing the stories of influential people like DeMar DeRozan with fantastic readers like you. My readers inspire me to write more so please do not hesitate to let me know what you thought by leaving a review! If you love books on life, basketball, or productivity, check out my website at claytongeoffreys.com to join my exclusive list where I let you know about my latest books. Aside from being the first to hear about my latest releases, you can also download a free copy of *33 Life Lessons: Success Principles, Career Advice & Habits of Successful People*. See you there!

*Clayton*

# References

[i] Mick, Hayley. "DeMar DeRozan: From Compton to Canada". *The Globe and Mail*. 5 November 2010. Web.

[ii] "DeMar DeRozan's Journey to Become the Face of the Raptors Franchise". *The Star*. 17 April 2015. Web.

[iii] Windhorst, Brian. "From the Shadow of Kobe, DeMar DeRozan Rises". *ESPN*. 6 December 2016. Web.

[iv] Medina, Mark. "DeMar DeRozan Has Stayed Loyal to LA and Toronto". *Daily News*. 22 July 2016. Web.

[v] "DeMarDeRozan". *NBADraft.net*

[vi] Mackenzie, Holly. "Growth of DeMar DeRozan Recognized by his Peers". *NBA.com*. 11 August 2014. Web.

[vii] Ganter, Mike. "NBA Scoring Leader DeMar DeRozan Reaps Benefits of 5:30am Workouts in Rio, 'Toughest' Summer of his Life". *National Post*. 14 November 2016. Web.

[viii] "DeMar DeRozan's Start for Toronto is Jordanesque". *LA Times*. 2 November 2016. Web.

[ix] Zillgitt, Jeff. "Evolution of an All-Star: Raptors guard DeMar DeRozan adds new wrinkle to offensive game". *USA Today*. 10 January 2018. Web.

[x] Herbert, James. "Raptors All-Star DeMar DeRozan shares secret to career season: Not giving a f---". *CBS Sports*. 1 February 2018. Web.

[xi] "DeMar DeRozan discusses trade to San Antonio Spurs, his memories of days with Toronto Raptors". *NBA.com*. 25 July 2018. Web.

[xii] Kelly, Cathal. "The DeMar DeRozan trade is a knife to the heart. And it had to be done". *The Globe and Mail*. 18 July 2018. Web.

[xiii] Hrinya, Greg. "Gregg Popovich looking forward to future with DeMar DeRozan". *AXS*. 19 July 2018. Web.

Made in the USA
Monee, IL
19 December 2021